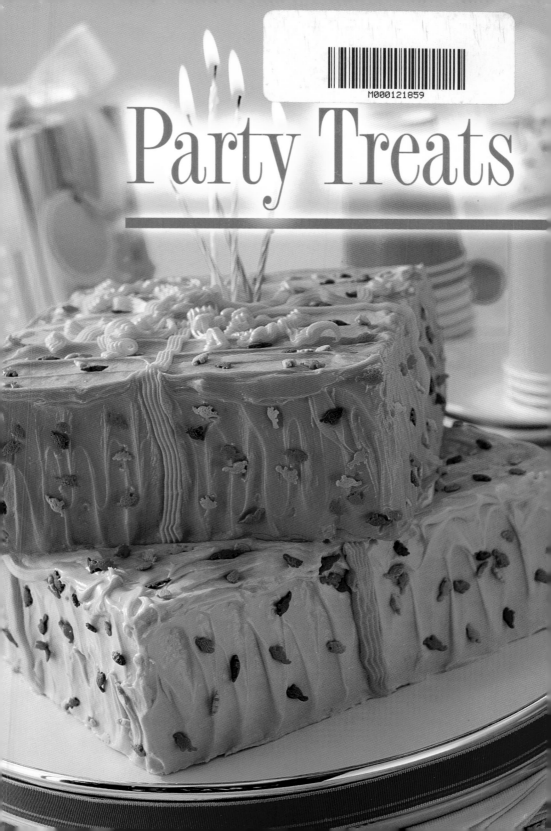

Party Treats

M000121859

Contents

Valentine's Day 4

Halloween 26

Christmas 46

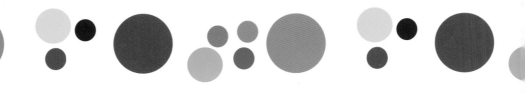

Valentine's Day

ICE CREAM SANDWICH HEARTS

Makes 8 sandwiches

2 packages (18 ounces each) refrigerated peanut butter cookie dough
2 tablespoons finely chopped peanuts
2 cups vanilla or chocolate ice cream, softened
Chocolate sauce or melted chocolate

1. Preheat oven to 350°F. Grease 15×10-inch jelly-roll pan. Let dough stand at room temperature about 15 minutes.

2. Press cookie dough evenly into prepared pan. Sprinkle with peanuts, pressing nuts in lightly. Bake 22 to 25 minutes or until set and golden brown. Cool completely in pan on wire rack.

3. Cut out 16 hearts with 3-inch heart-shaped cookie cutter. (Reserve scraps for snacking or discard.) Spoon ¼ cup ice cream onto 8 hearts; top with remaining hearts. Press each sandwich gently to spread ice cream to edges, scraping any excess from edges. To serve, place sandwiches on plates and drizzle with chocolate sauce.

Make-Ahead Time: up to 2 days
Final Prep Time: 10 minutes

BLACK & WHITE HEARTS

Makes about 3½ dozen cookies

  1 cup (2 sticks) butter, softened
  ¾ cup sugar
  1 package (3 ounces) cream cheese, softened
  1 egg
1½ teaspoons vanilla
  3 cups all-purpose flour
  1 cup semisweet chocolate chips
  2 tablespoons shortening

1. Beat butter, sugar, cream cheese, egg and vanilla in large bowl with electric mixer at medium speed until light and fluffy. Add flour; beat until well blended. Divide dough in half; wrap each half in plastic wrap. Refrigerate 2 hours or until firm.

2. Preheat oven to 375°F. Roll dough to ⅛-inch thickness on lightly floured surface. Cut dough with lightly floured 2-inch heart-shaped cookie cutter. Place cutouts 1 inch apart on ungreased cookie sheets. Bake 7 to 10 minutes or until edges are lightly browned. Remove immediately to wire racks; cool completely.

3. Melt chocolate chips and shortening in small saucepan over low heat 4 to 6 minutes or until melted. Dip half of each heart into melted chocolate. Refrigerate on cookie sheets or trays lined with waxed paper until chocolate is set. Store covered in refrigerator.

CHERRY-FILLED HEARTS

Makes 10 servings

½ package (17¼ ounces) frozen puff pastry sheets (1 sheet), thawed
1 egg yolk
1 teaspoon water
1 can (21 ounces) cherry pie filling
¼ teaspoon almond extract
1 cup hot fudge topping, heated
2½ cups whipped topping

1. Preheat oven to 400°F.

2. Unfold puff pastry sheet on lightly floured surface. Cut out 10 hearts from pastry with 3-inch heart-shaped cookie cutter. Place on ungreased baking sheet.

3. Combine egg yolk and water in small bowl; beat lightly with fork until well blended. Brush evenly onto pastry cutouts, covering completely. Bake 10 to 12 minutes or until golden brown. Cool on wire rack.

4. Meanwhile, combine pie filling and extract in medium saucepan. Cook over low heat, stirring occasionally, until heated through.

5. Spoon about 1 tablespoon fudge topping onto each of 10 dessert plates. Carefully split each heart horizontally in half. Place bottom halves of hearts on plates; top evenly with pie filling mixture and whipped topping. Replace top halves of hearts. Drizzle evenly with remaining fudge topping.

SAVORY SWEETIE PIES

Makes 15 appetizer servings

2 tablespoons all-purpose flour
1 teaspoon rubbed sage
¼ teaspoon salt
¼ teaspoon black pepper
½ pound boneless skinless chicken breasts, chopped
2 tablespoons butter or margarine
1 cup chicken broth
1 cup thawed frozen mixed vegetables
1 package (15 ounces) refrigerated pie crusts
1 egg yolk
1 teaspoon water

1. Preheat oven to 400°F. Lightly grease baking sheets.

2. Combine flour, sage, salt and pepper in medium bowl. Add chicken; toss to coat.

3. Melt butter in large skillet over medium heat. Add chicken and any remaining flour mixture; cook, stirring frequently, 5 minutes or until chicken is no longer pink in center. Stir in broth and vegetables. Reduce heat to low; simmer 5 to 8 minutes or until mixture is heated through.

4. Roll out 1 pie crust to 14-inch diameter on floured surface. Cut out 15 heart shapes with 3-inch heart-shaped cookie cutter. Repeat with second pie crust, rerolling pastry scraps if necessary, to make 30 hearts. Place half of hearts on prepared baking sheets; top each with heaping tablespoonful chicken mixture. Cover with remaining hearts; press edges together with tines of fork to seal.

5. Blend egg yolk and water in small bowl. Brush onto hearts. Bake 15 to 20 minutes or until golden brown.

SWEETEST HEART CAKE

Makes 12 to 16 servings

1 (8-inch) round cake, any flavor
1 (8-inch) square cake, any flavor
1 container (16 ounces) vanilla frosting, tinted pink with
    red food coloring
1½ cups flaked coconut, tinted pink to match frosting*
2 large red gumdrops
    Granulated sugar
1 large white gumdrop
    Red chewy fruit roll

*To tint coconut, combine small amount of food coloring (paste or liquid) with 1 teaspoon water in medium bowl. Add coconut and stir until evenly coated. Add more coloring, if needed.

1. Cut round cake in half to make two semi-circles.

2. Position square cake and semi-circles on large serving plate using photo as guide to make heart shape. Use some frosting to adhere pieces. Frost entire cake with remaining frosting. Sprinkle evenly with coconut.

3. Flatten 1 red gumdrop with rolling pin on lightly sugared surface to make small heart. Cut out heart shape with small cookie cutter. Repeat with remaining red gumdrop and white gumdrop. Place 3 gumdrop hearts on cake, overlapping slightly as shown in photo.

4. Cut chewy fruit roll into ½-inch strips. Tie strips into loose bow and place on cake.

CHOCOLATE AND PEANUT BUTTER HEARTS

Makes 4 dozen cookies

Chocolate Cookie Dough (page 14)
1 cup sugar
½ cup creamy peanut butter
½ cup shortening
1 egg
3 tablespoons milk
1 teaspoon vanilla
2 cups all-purpose flour
1 teaspoon baking powder
¼ teaspoon salt

1. Prepare and chill Chocolate Cookie Dough.

2. Beat sugar, peanut butter and shortening until fluffy. Add egg, milk and vanilla; mix well. Combine flour, baking powder and salt. Beat flour mixture into peanut butter mixture until well blended. Shape dough into disc. Wrap in plastic wrap; refrigerate 1 to 2 hours or until firm.

3. Preheat oven to 350°F. Grease cookie sheets. Roll out peanut butter dough on floured waxed paper to ⅛-inch thickness. Cut dough using 3-inch heart-shaped cookie cutters or smaller cookie cutters, if desired. Place cutouts on prepared cookie sheets. Repeat with chocolate dough.

4. Use smaller heart-shaped cookie cutters to cut small heart shapes from centers of large heart cutouts. Place small peanut butter hearts into large chocolate hearts; place small chocolate hearts into large peanut butter hearts. Press together lightly.

5. Bake 12 to 14 minutes or until edges are lightly browned. Remove to wire racks; cool completely.

continued on page 14

Chocolate and Peanut Butter Hearts, continued

CHOCOLATE COOKIE DOUGH

  1 cup (2 sticks) butter, softened
  1 cup sugar
  1 egg
  1 teaspoon vanilla
  2 ounces semisweet chocolate, melted
2¼ cups all-purpose flour
  1 teaspoon baking powder
  ¼ teaspoon salt

1. Beat butter and sugar in large bowl with electric mixer at medium-high speed until fluffy. Beat in egg and vanilla. Add melted chocolate; mix well.

2. Add flour, baking powder and salt; mix well. Cover; refrigerate about 2 hours or until firm.

SIMPLE MOLDED CANDY

Makes about 2 dozen candies

12 ounces confectionery coating
   Food coloring
   Valentine shaped molds

1. Melt confectionery coating in bowl over hot, not boiling, water stirring constantly. Add food coloring, a few drops at a time, until desired shade is reached.

2. Spoon into molds. Tap molds on countertop to remove bubbles. Refrigerate until firm. Bring to room temperature before unmolding to avoid cracking molds.

VARIATION: To make two-tone candies, choose molds with sections to allow for layering. Melt coating as directed. Spoon first layer of coating into molds; tap molds on countertop to remove bubbles. Refrigerate until firm. Spoon second layer into molds. Proceed as directed above.

LACY HEARTS CAKE

Makes 12 to 16 servings

Creamy White Frosting (page 17)
2 (8-inch) round cake layers
Base Frosting (page 17)
Red cinnamon candies
Red sugar

SUPPLIES

1 (10-inch) cake plate or round cake board, covered
Paper doily

1. Prepare Creamy White Frosting. If cake tops are rounded, trim horizontally with long serrated knife. Place one cake layer on cake plate. Spread about ½ cup Creamy White Frosting on cake; top with second cake layer.

2. Prepare Base Frosting. Frost entire cake with Base Frosting to seal in crumbs. Let stand until set. Frost entire cake with remaining Creamy White Frosting.

3. Cut out heart shape from doily. For overlapping heart decoration, place doily heart on cake top about ½ inch from left edge of cake. Place candies around left edge of pattern and about 1½ inches up right side from point, pressing gently into frosting.

4. Carefully lift off doily heart. Reposition doily heart on cake top, fitting left edge of pattern into space of first heart and about ½ inch from right edge of cake. (Be sure bottom points of hearts align.) Place candies around pattern to outline heart.

5. Sprinkle sugar over doily heart so sugar goes through holes, being careful to sprinkle only over doily. Brush sugar through holes with fingertip. Lift off doily heart, being careful to brush any sugar that clings to it.

6. Position left half of doily heart over left outlined heart and sprinkle with sugar. Lift off doily heart. Use toothpick to remove any sugar outside outlined hearts. Place single row of candies around bottom edge of cake, pressing gently into frosting.

CREAMY WHITE FROSTING

Makes enough to frost 2 (8-inch) round cake layers

½ cup shortening
6 cups sifted powdered sugar, divided
3 tablespoons milk
2 teaspoons clear vanilla extract
Additional milk*

For thinner frosting, use more milk and for thicker frosting use less milk.

1. Beat shortening in large bowl with electric mixer at medium speed until fluffy.

2. Gradually beat in 3 cups sugar until well blended and smooth. Carefully beat in 3 tablespoons milk and vanilla.

3. Gradually beat in remaining 3 cups sugar, adding more milk, 1 teaspoon at a time, as needed for good spreading consistency.

BASE FROSTING

Makes about 2 cups

3 cups powdered sugar, sifted
½ cup shortening
¼ cup milk
½ teaspoon vanilla
Additional milk

1. Beat sugar, shortening, ¼ cup milk and vanilla with electric mixer at medium speed in large bowl until smooth.

2. Add more milk, 1 teaspoon at a time, until frosting is thin consistency.

STRAWBERRY HEARTS

Makes about 2 dozen hearts

1 package (18 ounces) refrigerated sugar cookie dough
2 packages (8 ounces each) cream cheese, softened
⅔ cup powdered sugar
1 teaspoon vanilla
2 cups sliced fresh strawberries

1. Remove dough from wrapper and roll out. Cut out hearts with 2-inch heart-shaped cookie cutter. Bake as directed on package.

2. Combine cream cheese, powdered sugar and vanilla; mix well. Spread evenly onto cooled hearts. Top evenly with strawberries.

SWEETHEART PIZZETTES

Makes 16 appetizer servings

2 cups sour cream
½ package (1.4 ounces) dry vegetable soup mix (about ⅓ cup)
1 package (10 ounces) refrigerated pizza dough
3 tablespoons grated Parmesan cheese (optional)
½ cup chopped plum tomatoes

1. Combine sour cream and soup mix in small bowl; stir until well blended. Cover; refrigerate 2 to 3 hours or overnight.

2. Preheat oven to 425°F. Grease baking sheets; set aside.

3. Unroll pizza dough on floured surface; roll out to 15×13-inch rectangle. Using 2-inch heart-shaped cookie cutter, cut out 16 hearts. Cut out smaller hearts from any remaining scraps of dough, if desired. Place on prepared baking sheets; sprinkle evenly with Parmesan cheese.

4. Bake 8 to 10 minutes or until golden brown. Remove to wire racks to cool slightly. To serve, spread sour cream mixture evenly onto hearts and top evenly with tomatoes.

Top to bottom: Strawberry Hearts, Sweetheart Pizzettes and Savory Sweetie Pies (page 9)

CHOCOLATE-DIPPED STRAWBERRIES

Makes 12 strawberries

2 cups (11½ ounces) milk chocolate chips
1 tablespoon shortening
12 large strawberries with stems, rinsed and dried

1. Line baking sheet with waxed paper; set aside.

2. Melt chips with shortening in top of double boiler over hot (not boiling) water, stirring constantly.

3. Dip about half of each strawberry into chocolate. Remove excess chocolate by scraping bottom of strawberry across rim of pan. Place strawberries on prepared baking sheet. Let stand until set.

4. Store in refrigerator in airtight container between layers of waxed paper.

VARIATION: Melt 8 ounces white chocolate or pastel confectionery coating. Dip bottoms of dipped strawberries, leaving a portion of the milk chocolate coating showing.

TIP: Stir chopped dried fruits, raisins or nuts into any remaining chocolate; drop by tablespoonfuls onto a baking sheet lined with waxed paper. Let mixture set. Break into pieces.

VALENTINE SMOOTHIES

Makes 2 servings

1 cup vanilla yogurt
1 ripe banana, sliced
2 tablespoons strawberry jam
1 tablespoon honey or granulated sugar
3 or 4 drops red food coloring

1. Combine all ingredients in blender container; cover. Blend at high speed 20 seconds or until foamy.

2. Pour into 2 glasses and serve immediately. Garnish as desired.

Prep Time: 3 minutes

Bees have been producing honey for millions of years. A worker bee will toil for an entire lifetime to make $\frac{1}{12}$ teaspoon of honey (about 3 drops).

CUPID CAKES

Makes 12 servings

1 package (10 ounces) frozen strawberries, thawed and coarsely chopped
1 tablespoon powdered sugar
½ cup whipping cream, whipped
2 frozen all-butter pound cakes (10¾ ounces each), thawed
½ cup strawberry preserves

1. Drain strawberries; reserve 1 tablespoon juice. Gently combine strawberries, reserved juice and powdered sugar with whipped cream; set aside.

2. Cut each cake into 12 slices. Spread half of slices with about 1½ teaspoons preserves. Top with remaining slices to make sandwiches. Press each sandwich gently to spread preserves to edges, scraping any excess from edges. Place onto serving plates; top with whipped cream mixture.

Prep Time: 15 minutes

Cupid Cake

Halloween

FEET OF MEAT

Makes 8 to 10 servings

2½ pounds ground beef
1 clove garlic, minced
½ cup bread crumbs or oatmeal
½ cup milk or water
1 egg
1 envelope (1 ounce) dry onion soup mix
8 Brazil nuts or almonds
2 tablespoons barbecue sauce or ketchup

1. Preheat oven to 350°F. Combine ground beef, garlic, bread crumbs, milk, egg and onion soup mix in large bowl; stir until well blended. Reserve 1 cup meat mixture.

2. Divide remaining meat mixture in half; shape each half into 7×4-inch oval. Place ovals on rimmed baking sheet. Divide reserved 1 cup meat mixture into 8 balls; place 4 balls at end of each oval for toes. Press 1 nut into each toe for toenails. Brush meat loaves with barbecue sauce; bake 1½ hours or until meat thermometer registers 160°F.

TIP: When shaping feet, form "ankles" that have been "cut off" and fill them with dripping ketchup before serving for an especially gruesome effect!

MERINGUE BONE COOKIES

Makes 2 dozen cookies

1 ½ **cups sugar**
   Pinch of salt
 5 **egg whites at room temperature**
   Pinch of cream of tartar
 1 **teaspoon almond, vanilla, orange or lemon extract**

1. Preheat oven to 220°F. Line 2 cookie sheets with parchment paper. Prepare pastry bag with round #10 tip (about ⅜-inch diameter).

2. Combine sugar and salt in small bowl. Beat egg whites and cream of tartar in small bowl with electric mixer at low speed until soft peaks form. Gradually add sugar mixture, beating constantly. Beat until stiff peaks form and meringue is shiny and smooth. Add extract; beat just until blended.

3. Fill pastry bag with meringue. Pipe log 3 to 4 inches long. Pipe 2 balls on both ends of each log. Smooth any peaks with wet finger. Repeat with remaining meringue.

4. Bake 30 minutes; turn off heat. Leave cookies in oven overnight; do not open oven door.

Meringue Bone Cookies

SMASHED THUMBSTICKS WITH OILY DIPPING SAUCE

Makes 12 appetizers

THUMBSTICKS
1 package (11 ounces) refrigerated breadstick dough
12 sun-dried tomatoes, cut in half crosswise or jumbo pitted ripe olives, halved lengthwise
2 tablespoons olive oil
Dried dill or rosemary

DIPPING SAUCE
½ cup olive oil
2 tablespoons balsamic vinegar
1 teaspoon dried basil
½ teaspoon salt
¼ teaspoon black pepper

1. Preheat oven to 375°F. Unroll breadstick dough; separate each strip and cut in half crosswise. Place on 2 ungreased baking sheets. Place tomato half about ⅛ inch from top of each strip and press down firmly; shape ends to round out tip of thumb.

2. Gently press down on dough with knife in 2 places to resemble knuckles. Brush breadsticks with 2 tablespoons olive oil; sprinkle with basil. Bake 10 minutes or until light golden brown.

3. Meanwhile, combine dipping sauce ingredients in 1-pint jar; cover and shake until well blended. Serve with Thumbsticks.

BLOODSHOT EYEBALLS

Makes about 2½ dozen cookies

2¾ cups all-purpose flour
1 teaspoon baking soda
½ teaspoon salt
1 cup (2 sticks) butter, softened
¾ cup granulated sugar
¾ cup packed light brown sugar
2 eggs
1 teaspoon vanilla
1 container (16 ounces) white frosting
Green or blue gummy candy rings
1 tube (0.6 ounce) black decorating gel
1 tube (0.6 ounce) red decorating gel

1. Combine flour, baking soda and salt in small bowl. Beat together butter and sugars in large bowl with electric mixer on medium speed until light and fluffy. Beat in eggs, one at a time. Beat in vanilla. Add flour mixture gradually, mixing until well blended. Divide dough into two discs. Wrap in plastic wrap and chill at least 30 minutes.

2. Preheat oven to 375°F. Roll out dough on lightly floured surface to ⅛-inch thickness. Draw oval "eye" shape (about 4×2 inches) on piece of cardboard. Cut out shape and use as stencil for cutting cookie dough. Place cutouts 2 inches apart on ungreased cookie sheets. Bake 9 to 11 minutes or until golden brown. Transfer to wire racks; cool completely.

3. Spread frosting evenly over cooled cookies. Use candy rings to form an "iris" on each cookie. Fill in pupils and make eyelashes with black decorating gel. Decorate cookies with red decorating gel for bloodshot effect.

LOLLIPOP GARDEN BOUQUET

Makes 12 servings

(pictured on front cover)

1 package (18¼ ounces) carrot cake mix, plus
    ingredients to prepare mix
1 container (16 ounces) white frosting
    Green food coloring
½ cup crushed chocolate wafer cookies
    Green round hard sweet and sour candies
20 hard candy rings
    Green chewy fruit roll
6 to 10 lollipops

1. Prepare and bake cake mix according to package directions for one 8-inch round cake and one 9-inch round cake. Cool completely before frosting.

2. Blend frosting and food coloring in medium bowl until desired shade of green is reached. Place 8-inch cake layer on serving plate; spread top with frosting. Top with 9-inch cake layer; frost top and side of cake.

3. Sprinkle top of cake with cookie crumbs, leaving 1-inch border around edge of cake. Arrange round candies around edge of cake as shown on front cover. Press candy rings into side of bottom cake layer.

4. Use scissors to cut fruit roll into 2½-inch leaf shapes. Press leaves onto lollipop sticks; arrange lollipops in center of cake.

COFFIN COOKIES

Makes about 2 dozen sandwich cookies

1 package (about 16 ounces) refrigerated chocolate cookie dough*
Marshmallow Filling (recipe follows)
Colored sprinkles and sugars
Prepared white icing
Halloween decors

*If refrigerated chocolate cookie dough is unavailable, prepare your own. Place refrigerated sugar cookie dough and ¼ cup unsweetened cocoa powder in large bowl; beat with electric mixer at medium speed until well blended.

1. Draw and cut out pattern for coffin on cardboard using photo as guide. Preheat oven to 350°F. Remove dough from wrapper; divide dough in half. Reserve 1 half; wrap remaining half in plastic wrap and refrigerate.

2. Roll reserved dough on lightly floured surface to ⅛-inch thickness. Sprinkle with flour to minimize sticking, if necessary. Place pattern on cookie dough; cut dough around pattern with sharp knife. Repeat with remaining dough and scraps. Place cutouts 2 inches apart on ungreased cookie sheets.

3. Bake about 6 minutes or just until firm but not browned. Cool on cookie sheets 2 minutes. Remove to wire racks; cool completely.

4. Prepare Marshmallow Filling. Spread half of cookies with 2 teaspoons Filling; top with remaining cookies. Dip cookie sandwich edges in sprinkles. Decorate with icing and decors as desired.

MARSHMALLOW FILLING

Makes 1¾ cups

1 cup prepared vanilla frosting
¾ cup marshmallow creme

Mix frosting and marshmallow creme in small bowl until well blended.

SLOPPY GOBLINS

Makes 8 servings

1 pound ground beef
1 cup chopped onion
5 hot dogs, cut into ½-inch pieces
½ cup ketchup
¼ cup chopped dill pickle
¼ cup honey
¼ cup tomato paste
¼ cup prepared mustard
2 teaspoons cider vinegar
1 teaspoon Worcestershire sauce
8 hamburger buns
   Green and black olives
   Red bell pepper pieces
   Baby carrots

1. Cook beef and onion in large skillet 6 to 8 minutes over medium heat, stirring to break up meat. Drain fat. Stir in remaining ingredients except buns, olives, pepper slices and carrots. Cook, covered, 5 minutes or until heated through.

2. Spoon meat mixture onto bottoms of buns; cover with tops of buns. Serve with olives, pepper slices and carrots for decorating.

Sloppy Goblin

SPIDER CAKES

Makes 18 to 20 cupcakes

18 to 20 chocolate cupcakes
1 box (4-serving size) white chocolate pudding mix, prepared according
   to package directions and tinted green with food coloring
1 container (16 ounces) fudge frosting
   Paper Halloween baking cups
72 to 80 pieces black licorice, cut in half
36 to 40 red cinnamon candies
2 black licorice strings, cut into ¼-inch pieces for eyelashes (optional)

1. Poke small hole in bottom of each cupcake with toothpick. Snip off corner
of resealable food storage bag with scissors, making hole just large enough
for small, round piping tip to fit through. Place tip into opening. Spoon green
pudding into bag.

2. Insert piping tip into bottom of cupcake. Pipe some pudding gently and
slowly into each cake.

3. Frost tops and sides of cupcakes with frosting. Place each cupcake in slightly
flattened paper baking cup.

4. Place 4 pieces of licorice on each side of cupcake to form legs. Press in
cinnamon candies for eyes. Press licorice strings above cinnamon candies to
create eyelashes, if desired. Serve immediately.

*Create
a flavored fudge frosting
by adding ½ teaspoon almond or
mint extract.*

CREEPY COBWEBS

Makes 10 to 12 servings

4 to 5 cups vegetable oil
1 cup dry pancake mix
¾ cup plus 2 tablespoons milk
1 egg, beaten
½ cup powdered sugar
1 teaspoon ground cinnamon
½ teaspoon chili powder
Dipping Sauce (recipe follows)

1. Pour 1 inch of oil into heavy, deep 10-inch skillet. Heat oil to 350°F.

2. Combine pancake mix, milk, egg and 1 tablespoon oil in medium bowl. Do not overmix. Put 2 tablespoons batter into funnel or squeeze bottle; swirl into hot oil to form cobwebs. Cook in hot oil until bubbles form. Gently turn, using tongs and slotted spatula; fry 1 minute or until brown. Drain on cookie sheet lined with paper towels.

3. Repeat with remaining batter. If necessary, add more oil to maintain 1-inch depth and heat oil to 350°F again before frying more batter.

4. Meanwhile, mix powdered sugar, cinnamon and chili powder in small bowl. Sprinkle over cobwebs. Serve cobwebs with Dipping Sauce.

DIPPING SAUCE

Makes 1 cup

1 cup maple syrup
1 jalapeño pepper,* cored, seeded and minced

*Jalapeño peppers can sting and irritate the skin, so wear rubber gloves when handling peppers and do not touch your eyes.

Combine syrup and jalapeño in small saucepan. Simmer 5 minutes or until syrup is hot. Pour into heat-proof bowl.

LIME CHILLERS WITH BLOOD DRIPPINGS

Makes 10 servings

¼ cup honey or corn syrup
12 drops red food coloring
4 cups chilled pineapple juice
6 ounces frozen limeade concentrate
3 cups chilled ginger ale

1. Combine honey and food coloring in shallow pan; mix until well blended. Dip rims of 10 wine goblets into mixture one at a time, coating rims. Turn upright and let stand to allow mixture to drip down sides, resembling blood. Place paper towel around base of goblets to catch drips.

2. Combine pineapple juice and limeade in punch bowl. Stir until limeade dissolves; stir in ginger ale. Fill each wine goblet with lime chiller.

TOASTED CHEESE JACK-O'-LANTERNS

Makes 4 servings

3 tablespoons butter or margarine, softened
8 slices bread
4 slices Monterey Jack cheese
4 slices sharp Cheddar cheese

1. Preheat oven to 350°F. Spread butter on one side of each bread slice. Place bread, buttered side down, on ungreased cookie sheet.

2. Cut out shapes from 4 bread slices using paring knife to make jack-o'-lantern faces. Layer 1 slice Monterey Jack and 1 slice Cheddar on remaining 4 bread slices.

3. Bake 10 to 12 minutes or until cheese is melted. Remove from oven; place jack-o'-lantern bread slice on sandwiches. Serve immediately.

SKELETON COOKIES

Makes about 2 dozen cookies

30 to 40 drops black food coloring
1 package (about 16 ounces) refrigerated sugar cookie dough
   Skeleton or gingerbread man cookie cutters
1 tube white frosting

1. Knead food coloring into cookie dough on lightly floured waxed paper.* Wrap in plastic wrap and refrigerate 2 hours or until very firm.

2. Preheat oven to 350°F. Roll out dough between sheets of floured waxed paper to ⅛-inch thickness. Cut dough with cookie cutters. Bake 9 to 13 minutes or until edges are firm (centers will be somewhat soft). Cool 1 minute on cookie sheet; remove and cool completely on wire rack.

3. Draw skeleton figures on cookies with frosting as shown in photo.

Cookies will appear a shade or two lighter after baking. While kneading in the black food coloring, add a few more drops of coloring after the desired shade has been reached.

NOTE: The yield of this recipe is an approximation only and depends on the size of your cookie cutters.

Christmas

SNOWBALL BITES

Makes about 2½ dozen cookies

1 package (18 ounces) refrigerated sugar cookie dough
¾ cup all-purpose flour
2 tablespoons honey or maple syrup
1 cup chopped walnuts or pecans
Powdered sugar

1. Let dough stand at room temperature about 15 minutes.

2. Beat dough, flour and honey in large bowl with electric mixer at medium speed until well blended. Stir in walnuts. Shape dough into disc; wrap tightly in plastic wrap. Refrigerate dough at least 2 hours or up to 2 days.

3. Preheat oven to 350°F. Place powdered sugar in small bowl; set aside. Shape dough into ¾-inch balls; place 1½ inches apart on ungreased cookie sheets.

4. Bake 10 to 12 minutes or until bottoms are browned. Roll warm cookies in powdered sugar. Cool completely on wire racks. Just before serving, roll cookies in additional powdered sugar, if desired.

CHOCOLATE ALMOND CHERRY MIX

Makes 6 cups

2 cups toasted almonds*
2 cups red and green candy coated chocolate pieces
2 cups dried cherries

*To toast almonds, spread in a shallow baking pan. Bake in preheated 350°F oven 5 to 10 minutes or until golden brown, stirring frequently.

1. Combine all ingredients in large mixing bowl with wooden spoon.

2. To give as gifts or party favors, decorate individual resealable food storage bags or food-safe jars and fill with mix.

FESTIVE POPCORN TREATS

Makes 6 servings

6 cups popped popcorn
½ cup sugar
½ cup light corn syrup
¼ cup peanut butter
   Green food coloring
¼ cup red cinnamon candies

1. Line baking sheet with waxed paper.

2. Pour popcorn into large bowl. Combine sugar and corn syrup in medium saucepan. Bring to a boil over medium heat, stirring constantly; boil 1 minute. Remove from heat. Add peanut butter and green food coloring; stir until peanut butter is completely melted. Pour over popcorn; stir to coat well.

3. Lightly butter hands and shape popcorn mixture into cone shapes for trees. While trees are still warm, press red cinnamon candies into trees. Place on prepared baking sheet; let stand about 30 minutes or until firm.

Chocolate Almond Cherry Mix

HOLIDAY CANDY CANE TWISTS

Makes 8 servings

⅓ **cup sugar**
1 **tablespoon ground cinnamon**
1 **package (11 ounces) refrigerated breadstick dough**
3 **tablespoons butter or margarine, melted**
   Red decorating icing (optional)

1. Preheat oven to 350°F. Spray baking sheet with nonstick cooking spray.

2. Combine sugar and cinnamon in small bowl; mix well.

3. Separate dough; roll and stretch each piece of dough into 16-inch rope. Fold rope in half; twist ends together and form into candy cane shape on prepared baking sheet. Brush candy canes with butter; sprinkle with cinnamon-sugar.

4. Bake 12 to 15 minutes or until golden brown. Serve warm, either plain or decorated with red icing as shown in photo.

CHRISTMAS TREE ROLLS: Make cinnamon-sugar with green colored sugar instead of granulated sugar. Stretch dough into 16-inch ropes as directed. Cut off ½ inch from 1 end of each rope for tree trunk. Shape ropes into tree shapes on prepared baking sheet; add trunks. Brush with butter and sprinkle with green cinnamon-sugar. Bake as directed. Decorate with red cinnamon candies.

KITTENS AND MITTENS

Makes about 2 dozen cookies

Chocolate Cookie Dough (page 14)
4 cups powdered sugar
4 to 6 tablespoons milk
Assorted food colorings
Assorted candies

1. Preheat oven to 325°F. Grease cookie sheets.

2. Roll out dough on floured surface to ⅛-inch thickness. Cut out kitten and mitten shapes with cookie cutters. Place cutouts on prepared cookie sheets. Make holes in tops of cutouts with plastic straw, about ½ inch from top edges, if desired, to make ornaments.

3. Bake 8 to 10 minutes until edges begin to brown. Remove to wire racks; cool completely. (If necessary, push plastic straw through warm cookies to remake ornament holes.)

4. Combine 4 cups powdered sugar and 4 tablespoons milk in small bowl. Add 1 to 2 tablespoons additional milk as needed to make medium-thick, pourable glaze.

5. Place cookies on waxed paper-lined baking sheets. Spoon glaze into several small bowls; tint as desired with food colorings. Spoon glaze over cookies. Place remaining glaze in small resealable food storage bags. Cut tiny tip from corner of each bag. Pipe decorations and decorate with candies. Let stand until glaze is set.

6. Thread yarn or ribbon through holes to make ornaments, if desired.

GIANT GIFT BOXES

Makes 12 servings

(pictured on page 1)

1 package (18¼ ounces) chocolate or vanilla cake mix, plus ingredients
    to prepare mix
1 container (16 ounces) white frosting
  Green and orange food coloring
  Yellow decorating icing
  Candy sprinkles

1. Prepare and bake cake mix according to package directions for two
8- or 9-inch square cakes. Cool completely before frosting.

2. Blend half of frosting and green food coloring in medium bowl until
desired shade is reached. Repeat with remaining frosting and orange food
coloring.

3. Place one cake layer on serving plate; frost top and sides with green frosting.
Pipe stripe of icing on each side to resemble ribbon. Let frosting set before
adding second cake layer. Place second cake layer slightly off-center and rotated
45 degrees from bottom layer using photo as guide. Frost top and sides with
orange frosting. Pipe stripe of icing on each side to resemble ribbon.

4. Pipe additional icing on top of cake for bow and streamers as shown
in photo. Decorate cake with candy sprinkles.

Kids' Cake Mix

Contents

Everyday Favorites 58

Animal Fun 76

Holiday Treats 94

Everyday Favorites

CRUNCHY PEACH SNACK CAKE

Makes 9 servings

1 package (9 ounces) yellow cake mix without pudding in the mix
1 container (6 ounces) peach-flavor yogurt
1 egg
¼ cup peach fruit spread
¾ cup square whole grain oat cereal with cinnamon, slightly crushed
  Whipped cream (optional)

1. Place rack in center of oven; preheat oven to 350°F. Lightly grease 8-inch square baking pan.

2. Combine cake mix, yogurt and egg in medium bowl. Beat with electric mixer at low speed about 1 minute or until blended. Increase speed to medium; beat 1 to 2 minutes or until smooth.

3. Spread batter into prepared pan. Drop fruit spread by ½ teaspoonfuls over cake batter. Sprinkle with cereal.

4. Bake 25 minutes or until toothpick inserted into center of cake comes out clean. Cool on wire rack. Serve with whipped cream, if desired.

PEANUT BUTTER & MILK CHOCOLATE CUPCAKES

Makes 24 cupcakes

1 package (18¼ ounces) butter recipe yellow cake mix with pudding in
    the mix, plus ingredients to prepare mix
½ cup creamy peanut butter
¼ cup (½ stick) butter
2 bars (3½ ounces each) high-quality milk chocolate, broken into small
    pieces
¼ cup (½ stick) unsalted butter, cut into small chunks
¼ cup heavy cream
    Dash salt
    Peanut butter chips

1. Preheat oven to 350°F. Line 24 standard (2½-inch) muffin cups with paper baking cups.

2. Prepare cake mix according to package directions with ½ cup peanut butter and ¼ cup (½ stick) butter (instead of ½ cup butter called for in package directions). Fill muffin cups evenly with batter.

3. Bake 24 to 26 minutes or until light golden brown and toothpick inserted into centers comes out clean. Cool cupcakes in pans on wire racks 5 minutes. Remove from pans to racks; cool completely.

4. Combine chocolate, unsalted butter, cream and salt in small, heavy saucepan. Heat over very low heat, stirring constantly, just until butter and chocolate melt. Mixture should be warm, not hot. Immediately spoon about 1 tablespoon chocolate glaze over each cupcake, spreading to cover top. Sprinkle with peanut butter chips.

SWEET MYSTERIES

Makes 3 dozen cookies

  1 package (18¼ ounces) yellow cake mix with pudding in the mix
½ cup (1 stick) unsalted butter, softened
  1 egg yolk
  1 cup ground pecans
36 milk chocolate candy kisses
    Powdered sugar

1. Preheat oven to 300°F.

2. Beat half of cake mix and butter in large bowl with electric mixer at high speed until blended. Add egg yolk and remaining cake mix; beat at medium speed just until dough forms. Add pecans; beat just until blended.

3. Shape rounded tablespoon of dough around each candy, making sure candy is completely covered. Place 1 inch apart on ungreased cookie sheets.

4. Bake 20 to 25 minutes or until firm and just beginning to turn golden. Let cookies stand on cookie sheets 10 minutes. Transfer to wire racks set over waxed paper; dust with powdered sugar.

Add to the flavor of these delicious cookies by using white and milk chocolate striped candy kisses instead of the plain milk chocolate candy kisses.

DOUBLE CHOCOLATE CHIP SNACK CAKE

Makes 8 to 10 servings

(pictured on back cover)

1 package (18¼ ounces) devil's food cake mix with pudding
   in the mix, divided
2 eggs
½ cup water
¼ cup vegetable oil
½ teaspoon cinnamon
1 cup semisweet chocolate chips, divided
¼ cup packed brown sugar
2 tablespoons butter, melted
¾ cup white chocolate chips

1. Preheat oven to 350°F. Grease 9-inch round cake pan. Reserve ¾ cup dry cake mix; set aside.

2. Combine remaining cake mix, eggs, water, oil and cinnamon in large bowl; beat with electric mixer at medium speed 2 minutes. Remove ½ cup batter; reserve for another use.* Spread remaining batter in prepared pan; sprinkle with ½ cup semisweet chocolate chips.

3. Combine reserved cake mix and brown sugar in medium bowl. Stir in butter and remaining ½ cup semisweet chocolate chips; mix well. Sprinkle mixture over batter in pan.

4. Bake 35 to 40 minutes or until toothpick inserted into center comes out clean and cake springs back when lightly touched.

5. Place white chocolate chips in resealable food storage bag; seal bag. Microwave on HIGH 10 seconds and knead bag gently. Repeat until chips are melted. Cut off ¼ inch from corner of bag with scissors; drizzle chocolate over cake. Cool cake on wire rack before cutting into wedges.

*If desired, extra batter can be used for cupcakes: Pour batter into two foil or paper baking cups placed on baking sheet; bake at 350°F 18 to 20 minutes or until toothpick inserted into centers comes out clean.

CINNAMON CEREAL CRISPIES

Makes about 5 dozen cookies

½ cup granulated sugar

2 teaspoons ground cinnamon, divided

1 package (18¼ ounces) white or yellow cake mix with pudding in the mix

½ cup water

⅓ cup vegetable oil

1 egg

2 cups crisp rice cereal

1 cup cornflakes

1 cup raisins

1 cup chopped nuts (optional)

1. Preheat oven to 350°F. Lightly spray cookie sheets with nonstick cooking spray. Combine sugar and 1 teaspoon cinnamon in small bowl.

2. Beat cake mix, water, oil, egg and remaining 1 teaspoon cinnamon in large bowl with electric mixer at medium speed 1 minute. Gently stir in rice cereal, cornflakes, raisins and nuts, if desired, until well blended.

3. Drop batter by rounded tablespoonfuls 2 inches apart onto prepared cookie sheets. Sprinkle lightly with half of cinnamon-sugar mixture.

4. Bake about 15 minutes or until lightly browned. Sprinkle cookies with remaining cinnamon-sugar mixture after baking. Remove to wire racks; cool completely.

SUNSHINE SANDWICHES

Makes 30 cookies

⅓ cup coarse or granulated sugar
¾ cup (1½ sticks) plus 2 tablespoons butter, softened, divided
1 egg
2 tablespoons grated lemon peel
1 package (18¼ ounces) lemon cake mix with pudding in the mix
¼ cup yellow cornmeal
2 cups sifted powdered sugar
2 to 3 tablespoons lemon juice
2 drops yellow food coloring (optional)

1. Preheat oven to 375°F. Place coarse sugar in shallow bowl.

2. Beat ¾ cup butter in large bowl with electric mixer at medium speed until fluffy. Add egg and lemon peel; beat 30 seconds. Add cake mix, one third at a time, beating at low speed after each addition until combined. Stir in cornmeal. (Dough will be stiff.)

3. Shape dough into 1-inch balls; roll in coarse sugar to coat. Place 2 inches apart on ungreased cookie sheets. Bake 8 to 9 minutes or until bottoms begin to brown. Let cookies stand on cookie sheets 1 minute. Remove to wire racks; cool completely.

4. Meanwhile, beat powdered sugar and remaining 2 tablespoons butter in small bowl with electric mixer at low speed until blended. Gradually add enough lemon juice to reach spreading consistency. Stir in food coloring, if desired.

5. Spread 1 slightly rounded teaspoon of frosting on bottom of one cookie. Top with second cookie, bottom side down. Repeat with remaining cookies and frosting. Store covered at room temperature for up to 24 hours or freeze.

TOPSY-TURVY BANANA CRUNCH CAKE

Makes 9 servings

⅓ cup uncooked old-fashioned oats

3 tablespoons packed brown sugar

1 tablespoon all-purpose flour

¼ teaspoon ground cinnamon

2 tablespoons butter

2 tablespoons chopped pecans

1 package (9 ounces) yellow cake mix without pudding in the mix

½ cup sour cream

½ cup mashed banana (about 1 medium)

1 egg, slightly beaten

½ cup pecan halves (optional)

1. Preheat oven to 350°F. Lightly grease 8-inch square baking pan.

2. Combine oats, brown sugar, flour and cinnamon in small bowl. Cut in butter with pastry blender or 2 knives until crumbly. Stir in chopped pecans.

3. Combine cake mix, sour cream, banana and egg in medium bowl. Beat with electric mixer at low speed about 1 minute or until blended. Increase speed to medium; beat 1 to 2 minutes or until smooth. Spoon half of batter into prepared pan; sprinkle with half of oat topping. Top with remaining batter and oat topping. Sprinkle with pecan halves, if desired.

4. Bake 25 to 30 minutes or until toothpick inserted into center comes out clean. Cool completely on wire rack.

MARSHMALLOW FUDGE SUNDAE CUPCAKES

Makes 20 cupcakes

1 package (18¼ ounces) chocolate cake mix, plus
   ingredients to prepare mix
2 packages (4 ounces each) waffle bowls
40 large marshmallows
1 jar (8 ounces) hot fudge topping
1¼ cups whipped topping
¼ cup colored sprinkles
1 jar (10 ounces) maraschino cherries

1. Preheat oven to 350°F. Lightly spray 20 standard (2½-inch) muffin cups with nonstick cooking spray.

2. Prepare cake mix according to package directions. Spoon batter into prepared cups, filling two-thirds full. Bake 20 minutes or until toothpick inserted into centers come out clean. Cool in pans on wire racks about 10 minutes.

3. Place one cupcake in each waffle bowl. Place waffle bowls on baking sheets. Top each cupcake with 2 marshmallows and return to oven 2 minutes or until marshmallows are slightly softened.

4. Remove lid from fudge topping; heat in microwave on HIGH 10 seconds or until softened. Spoon 2 teaspoons fudge topping over each cupcake. Top with 1 tablespoon whipped topping, sprinkles and cherry.

Maraschino cherries are sweet cherries that are pitted, soaked in sugar syrup, flavored and then dyed a vivid red or green.

OOEY-GOOEY CARAMEL PEANUT BUTTER BARS

Makes 24 bars

1 package (18¼ ounces) yellow cake mix without pudding in the mix
1 cup uncooked quick oats
⅔ cup creamy peanut butter
1 egg, slightly beaten
2 tablespoons milk
1 package (8 ounces) cream cheese, softened
1 jar (12¼ ounces) caramel ice cream topping
1 cup semisweet chocolate chips

1. Preheat oven to 350°F. Lightly grease 13×9-inch baking pan.

2. Combine cake mix and oats in large bowl. Cut in peanut butter with pastry blender or 2 knives until mixture is crumbly.

3. Blend egg and milk in small bowl. Add to peanut butter mixture; stir just until combined. Reserve 1½ cups mixture. Press remaining peanut butter mixture into prepared pan.

4. Beat cream cheese in small bowl with electric mixer at medium speed until fluffy. Add caramel topping; beat just until combined. Carefully spread over peanut butter layer in pan. Break up reserved peanut butter mixture into small pieces; sprinkle over cream cheese layer. Top with chocolate chips.

5. Bake about 30 minutes or until nearly set in center. Cool completely in pan on wire rack.

BLACK AND WHITE SANDWICH COOKIES

Makes 3 dozen sandwich cookies

1 package (18¼ ounces) chocolate cake mix with pudding in the mix

1½ cups (3 sticks) unsalted butter, softened, divided

2 egg yolks, divided

½ to ¾ cup milk, divided

1 package (18¼ ounces) butter recipe yellow cake mix with pudding in the mix

4 cups powdered sugar

¼ teaspoon salt

1. Preheat oven to 325°F.

2. For chocolate cookies, place half of chocolate cake mix in large bowl. Add ½ cup (1 stick) butter; beat with electric mixer at high speed until well blended. Add 1 egg yolk and remaining cake mix; beat just until dough forms. Beat in 1 to 2 tablespoons milk if dough is too crumbly.

3. Shape dough into 36 balls, using about 1 tablespoon dough for each cookie. Place 2 inches apart on ungreased cookie sheets; flatten slightly. Bake 20 minutes or until cookies are firm. Let cookies stand on cookie sheets 5 minutes. Remove to wire racks; cool completely.

4. For vanilla cookies, place half of yellow cake mix in large bowl. Add ½ cup (1 stick) butter; beat with electric mixer at high speed until well blended. Add remaining egg yolk and cake mix; beat just until dough forms. Beat in 1 to 2 tablespoons milk if dough is too crumbly.

5. Shape dough into 36 balls, using about 1 tablespoon dough for each cookie. Place 2 inches apart on ungreased cookie sheets; flatten slightly. Bake 20 minutes or until cookies are firm. Let cookies stand on cookie sheets 5 minutes. Remove to wire racks; cool completely.

6. Cut remaining ½ cup (1 stick) butter into small pieces. Beat butter, powdered sugar, salt and 6 tablespoons milk in large bowl with electric mixer until light and fluffy. Add additional 2 tablespoons milk if necessary for more spreadable frosting. Spread frosting on flat sides of chocolate cookies, using about 1 tablespoon per cookie. Top with vanilla cookies.

Animal Fun

LADYBUG

Makes 12 servings

1 package (18¼ ounces) white cake mix, plus
    ingredients to prepare mix
1 container (16 ounces) vanilla frosting
¼ cup red raspberry preserves
    Red decorating sugar
    Candy-coated chocolate pieces
8 dark chocolate discs or mint chocolate cookies
    String licorice and assorted gumdrops
    Large peppermint patty
1 cup flaked coconut tinted green with food coloring*

*To tint coconut, combine small amount of food coloring (paste or liquid) with 1 teaspoon water in medium bowl. Add coconut and stir until evenly coated. Add more coloring, if needed.

1. Prepare and bake cake mix according to package directions for two 9-inch round cakes. Cool completely.

2. Place one cake layer on serving plate; spread with frosting. Spread raspberry preserves over frosting to within ½ inch of edge. Top with second cake layer; frost top and side of cake with remaining frosting.

3. Sprinkle top of cake with sugar; decorate with chocolate pieces and discs as shown in photo. Create face with licorice and gumdrops; attach to mint patty with small amounts of frosting. Place patty on cake. Press coconut onto side of cake.

FLUTTER AWAY

Makes 12 servings

1 package (18¼ ounces) white or chocolate cake mix, plus ingredients to
    prepare mix
1 container (16 ounces) vanilla frosting
    Food coloring, any color
1 filled rolled wafer cookie, any flavor
    Gumdrops, gummy hearts and small round sugar candies

1. Preheat oven to 350°F. Grease and flour two 9-inch round cake pans.

2. Prepare cake mix according to package directions. Bake 28 to 31 minutes or
until toothpick inserted into centers comes out clean. Cool completely before
frosting.

3. Blend frosting and food coloring in medium bowl until desired shade is
reached. Cut each cake layer crosswise in half; place two halves on serving
plate, cut sides facing out. Frost top of cake layers; top each half with remaining
halves. Using serrated knife, cut triangles two-thirds down from top of each
half to form butterfly wings as shown in photo.

4. Frost top and sides of cake with remaining frosting. Place wafer cookie
between cake halves to form butterfly body. Decorate wings with candies as
desired.

MISS PINKY THE PIG CUPCAKES

Makes 24 cupcakes

2 jars (10 ounces each) maraschino cherries, well drained
1 package (18¼ ounces) white cake mix without pudding in the mix
1 cup sour cream
½ cup vegetable oil
3 egg whites
¼ cup water
½ teaspoon almond extract
   Red food coloring
1 container (16 ounces) cream cheese frosting
48 small gumdrops
   Mini candy-coated chocolate pieces, mini chocolate chips, white decorating icing and colored sugar

1. Preheat oven to 350°F. Line 24 standard (2½-inch) muffin cups with paper baking cups. Spray 24 mini (1¾-inch) muffin cups with nonstick cooking spray. Pat cherries dry with paper towels. Place in food processor; process 4 to 5 seconds or until finely chopped.

2. Beat cake mix, sour cream, oil, egg whites, water and almond extract in large bowl with electric mixer at low speed about 1 minute or until blended. Increase speed to medium; beat 1 to 2 minutes or until smooth. Stir in cherries. Spoon 2 slightly rounded tablespoons batter into prepared standard muffin cups, filling each about half full. (Cups will be slightly less full than normal.) Spoon remaining batter into mini muffin cups, filling each about one-third full.

3. Bake standard cupcakes 14 to 18 minutes and mini cupcakes 7 to 9 minutes or until toothpick inserted into centers comes out clean. Cool cupcakes in pans on wire racks 5 minutes. Remove from pans to racks; cool completely.

4. Blend food coloring into frosting, a few drops at a time, until desired shade of pink is reached. Frost tops of larger cupcakes. Press top of small cupcake onto one side of each large cupcake top. Frost small cupcakes. Place gumdrops between two layers of waxed paper. Flatten to ⅛-inch thickness with rolling pin; cut out triangles. Arrange gumdrops on cupcakes for ears; complete faces with remaining ingredients.

TEDDY BEAR

Makes 16 servings

1 package (18¼ ounces) chocolate cake mix, plus ingredients to
    prepare mix
1 container (16 ounces) chocolate frosting
4 cupcakes
2 heart-shaped gummy candies *or* ¼ cup white chocolate chips
1 package (12 ounces) mini semisweet chocolate chips
2 large white gumdrops
2 small black round gummy candies
¼ cup butterscotch or peanut butter chips
1 red gumdrop or small round gummy candy
    Black and red licorice strings, cut into small pieces

1. Prepare and bake cake mix according to package directions for two 8- or 9-inch round cakes. Cool completely before frosting.

2. Place one cake layer on serving plate; top with small amount of frosting. Top with second cake layer; frost top and side. Stack two cupcakes next to cake to resemble ear; frost cupcakes. Place heart-shaped gummy candies in center of ears. Press chocolate chips into side and top edges of cake and cupcakes.

3. Flatten two white gumdrops with rolling pin; arrange on cake to resemble eyes. Use small dab of frosting to attach black candies to white gumdrops. Mound butterscotch chips below eyes to resemble muzzle. Decorate face with candy and licorice strips as desired.

DOODLE BUG CUPCAKES

Makes 24 cupcakes

1 package (18¼ ounces) white cake mix without pudding in the mix
1 cup sour cream
3 eggs
⅓ cup vegetable oil
⅓ cup water
1 teaspoon vanilla
1½ cups prepared cream cheese frosting
   Red, yellow, blue and green food coloring
   Red licorice strings, cut into 2-inch pieces
   Assorted round decorating candies

1. Preheat oven to 350°F. Line 24 standard (2½-inch) muffin cups with paper baking cups.

2. Beat cake mix, sour cream, eggs, oil, water and vanilla in large bowl with electric mixer at low speed about 1 minute or until blended. Increase speed to medium; beat 1 to 2 minutes or until smooth. Spoon batter evenly into prepared muffin cups, filling two-thirds full.

3. Bake about 20 minutes or until toothpick inserted into centers comes out clean. Cool cupcakes in pans on wire racks 5 minutes. Remove from pans to racks; cool completely.

4. Divide frosting evenly between 4 small bowls. Add food coloring to each bowl, one drop at a time, to reach desired shades; stir each frosting until well blended. Frost tops of cupcakes.

5. Use toothpick to make three small holes on opposite sides of each cupcake. Insert licorice piece into each hole for legs. Decorate tops of cupcakes with assorted candies.

KITTY KAT

Makes 12 servings

1 package (18¼ ounces) carrot cake mix, plus ingredients to prepare mix
1 container (16 ounces) cream cheese frosting
   Red and yellow food coloring
2 cupcakes
¼ cup chocolate sprinkles
   Assorted round and heart-shaped candies
   Black licorice string

1. Preheat oven to 350°F. Prepare and bake cake mix according to package directions for two 8- or 9-inch round cakes. Cool completely.

2. Blend frosting and red and yellow food coloring in medium bowl until desired shade of orange is reached. Place one cake layer on serving plate; spread with frosting. Top with second cake layer; frost top and side of cake.

3. Cut ⅜ inch from 3 sides of each cupcake to create triangles to resemble ears. Position ears next to cake and frost. Use tines of fork to make frosting resemble fur as shown in photo. Scatter sprinkles around edge of cake and in center of ears.

4. Decorate cat face with assorted candies. Cut licorice string into 2-inch lengths for mouth. Position candles on cake to resemble whiskers or use additional licorice strings.

Before attempting to remove a cake from its pan, carefully run a table knife or narrow metal spatula around the outside of the cake to loosen.

UNDER THE SEA

Makes 12 servings

1 package (18¼ ounces) chocolate cake mix, plus ingredients
    to prepare mix
1 container (16 ounces) vanilla frosting
    Blue food coloring
    Assorted sea life gummy candies
    Rock candy

1. Preheat oven to 350°F. Grease and flour 13×9-inch cake pan.

2. Prepare cake mix according to package directions. Bake in prepared pan 32 to 35 minutes or until toothpick inserted into center comes out clean. Cool cake in pan about 20 minutes. Remove from pan to wire rack; cool completely.

3. Blend frosting and food coloring in medium bowl until desired shade of blue is reached. Place cake on serving platter; frost top and sides of cake. Decorate cake with gummy candies and rock candy as desired.

BUTTERFLY CUPCAKES

Makes 24 cupcakes

(pictured on front cover)

1 package (18¼ ounces) cake mix, any flavor, plus ingredients
    to prepare mix
1 container (16 ounces) white frosting
   Blue food coloring
   Candy-coated chocolate pieces
   Colored sugar
   Red licorice strings, cut into 4-inch pieces

1. Preheat oven to 350°F. Lightly spray 24 standard (2½-inch) muffin cups with nonstick cooking spray.

2. Prepare cake mix according to package directions. Spoon batter into prepared muffin cups, filling two-thirds full.

3. Bake about 20 minutes or until toothpick inserted into centers comes out clean. Cool cupcakes in pans on wire racks about 10 minutes. Remove from pans to racks; cool completely.

4. Blend food coloring into frosting, one drop at a time, until desired shade of blue is reached.

5. Cut cupcakes in half. Place cupcake halves together, cut sides out, to resemble butterfly wings. Frost and decorate with chocolate pieces and colored sugar as desired. Snip each end of licorice pieces to form antennae; place in center of each cupcake.

PUPCAKES

Makes 24 cupcakes

1 package (18¼ ounces) chocolate cake mix, plus ingredients
    to prepare mix
½ cup (1 stick) butter, softened
4 cups powdered sugar
¼ to ½ cup half-and-half or milk
    Red and yellow chewy fruit snacks
    Candy-coated chocolate pieces
    Assorted colored jelly beans

1. Preheat oven to 350°F. Line 24 standard (2½-inch) muffin cups with paper baking cups.

2. Prepare cake mix and bake in prepared muffin cups according to package directions. Cool cupcakes in pans on wire racks 15 minutes. Remove from pans to racks; cool completely.

3. Beat butter in large bowl with electric mixer until creamy. Gradually add powdered sugar to form very stiff frosting, scraping down side of bowl occasionally. Gradually add half-and-half until frosting is of desired consistency. Frost tops of cupcakes.

4. Cut out ear and tongue shapes from fruit snacks with scissors; arrange on cupcakes, pressing into frosting. Add chocolate pieces and jelly beans to create eyes and noses.

PONIES IN THE MEADOW

Makes 12 servings

1 package (18¼ ounces) cake mix, any flavor, plus
    ingredients to prepare mix
1 cup flaked coconut tinted green with food coloring*
    Green food coloring
1 container (16 ounces) white frosting
    Pretzel sticks
2 small plastic ponies

To tint coconut, combine small amount of food coloring (paste or liquid) with 1 teaspoon water in large bowl. Add coconut and stir until evenly coated. Add more coloring, if needed.

1. Preheat oven to 350°F. Prepare and bake cake mix according to package directions in two 8-inch square pans. Cool in pans on wire racks 10 minutes. Remove to racks; cool completely.

2. Blend frosting and food coloring in medium bowl until desired shade of green is reached. Place one cake layer on serving plate; spread with ½ cup frosting. Top with second cake layer; frost top and sides of cake with remaining frosting.

3. Scatter coconut over top of cake and around edges of serving plate. Stand pretzel sticks around edges of cake to create fence; arrange ponies as desired.

TIP: Additional decorations can be added to the cake. Arrange candy rocks or brown jelly beans to create a path. Use the star tip on red or yellow decorating icing to create flowers in the meadow.

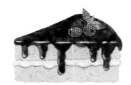

Holiday Treats

TIME TO PARTY

Makes 12 servings

1 package (18¼ ounces) carrot cake mix with pudding
in the mix, plus ingredients to prepare mix
1 container (16 ounces) cream cheese frosting
Food coloring (optional)
12 chocolate or multi-colored candy discs
Candy-coated chocolate and peanut pieces
Tube decorating icing
Letter candles (optional)

1. Preheat oven to 350°F. Prepare cake mix and bake in two 9-inch round cake pans according to package directions. Cool completely.

2. Blend frosting and food coloring, if desired, in medium bowl until desired shade is reached. Place one cake layer on serving plate; spread with about ½ cup frosting. Top with second cake layer; frost top and side of cake with remaining frosting.

3. Arrange chocolate candies on cake in position of clock numbers. Pipe numbers onto each chocolate candy with icing. Create hands of clock using chocolate and peanut pieces; place on cake at desired time. Press additional chocolate pieces around base of cake as shown in photo. Spell out "Time to Party" on cake with letter candles, if desired.

LUCK O' THE IRISH CUPCAKES

Makes 24 cupcakes

1 package (18¼ ounces) cake mix, any flavor, plus ingredients
    to prepare mix
1 container (16 ounces) white frosting
1 tube (4¼ ounces) green decorating icing with tip
  Green and orange sprinkles, decors and sugars

1. Preheat oven to 350°F. Line 24 standard (2½-inch) muffin cups with decorative paper baking cups. Prepare cake mix according to package directions. Spoon batter into prepared muffin cups, filling two-thirds full.

2. Bake 15 to 20 minutes or until toothpick inserted into centers comes out clean. Cool in pans on wire racks 10 minutes. Remove cupcakes to racks; cool completely.

3. Frost cupcakes. Use icing to pipe Irish words or shamrock designs onto cupcakes. Decorate with sprinkles, decors and sugars as desired.

To easily fill muffin cups, place batter in a 4-cup glass measure. Fill each cup two-thirds full, using a plastic spatula to control the flow of the batter.

FIRECRACKERS FOR THE FOURTH

Makes 30 servings

3 packages (18¼ ounces each) cake mix, any flavor, with pudding in the
    mix, plus ingredients to prepare mixes

3 empty 6-ounce aluminum cans, washed, dried and both ends removed

2 cups strawberry fruit spread

3 containers (16 ounces each) vanilla frosting

   Red and blue paste food coloring

   Black licorice string

1 tube (4¼ ounces) white decorating icing with tips

1. Prepare cake mixes according to package directions. Reserve 1 cup batter.
Divide remaining batter among two 9-inch square baking pans and four 8-inch
square baking pans. Bake according to package directions. Grease and flour
cans; cover one end with aluminum foil. Pour ⅓ cup reserved cake batter into
each can; place on baking sheet. Bake cans 18 to 20 minutes. Cool in pans and
cans 10 minutes. Remove to wire racks; cool completely. Wrap in plastic wrap;
freeze overnight.

2. Trim two 8-inch cakes to 5-inch squares. Spread one 5-inch cake, one
8-inch cake and one 9-inch cake with ⅓ cup fruit spread each; top each
with remaining same-sized cake.

3. Place 1½ containers of frosting in medium bowl; tint with red food
coloring until desired shade of red is reached. Place ½ container of frosting in
small bowl; tint with blue food coloring until desired shade of blue is reached.
Frost sides of 9-inch cake with red frosting; frost top 1-inch edges with white
frosting. Top with 8-inch cake, turning at angle to the right. Frost 1 side of
8-inch cake plus 1-inch edge on top of same side of cake with blue frosting;
frost remaining sides and 1-inch border on top of cake with white frosting. Top
with 5-inch cake, also twisting to the right at same angle. Frost 1 side of 5-inch
cake with blue frosting; frost remaining sides with red frosting. Frost can cakes
one each with red, white and blue frosting.

4. Add firecrackers to cake top, cutting ends at angles as necessary. Place
remaining white and blue frostings in small resealable food storage bags. Cut
off tiny corner of each bag; pipe onto firecrackers as desired. Place small piece
of licorice in each firecracker for fuse. Pipe border around base and top of cake
and up sides with white icing.

JACK-O'-LANTERN GINGERBREAD

Makes 12 servings

2 packages (14½ ounces each) gingerbread cake mix, plus
    ingredients to prepare mixes
3 teaspoons grated orange peel
  Powdered sugar or frosting
2 orange gumdrops
1 green gumdrop

1. Prepare cake mixes according to package directions, adding orange peel to batter. Bake in greased 11-inch molded jack-o'-lantern pan about 35 minutes or until toothpick inserted in center comes out clean.

2. Cool 10 minutes in pan on wire rack. Remove cake to rack; cool completely.

3. Cut out pumpkin face from clean sheet of paper. Place over top of cake; dust with powdered sugar. Brush any excess sugar through holes with fingertip. Lift off paper, being careful not to let any excess sugar sprinkle outside of pumpkin face. Use orange gumdrops for eyes and roll out green gumdrop to make stem of pumpkin.

LIBERTY'S TORCHES

Makes 26 servings

1 package (18¼ ounces) cake mix, any flavor, plus ingredients
    to prepare mix
26 flat-bottomed ice cream cones
26 red, yellow and orange chewy fruit rolls
    Yellow food coloring
1 container (16 ounces) white frosting

1. Preheat oven to 350°F. Stand 24 ice cream cones in 13×9-inch pan and remaining 2 cones in muffin cups or in small loaf pan. (Or, place all cones in muffin cups.)

2. Prepare cake mix according to package directions. Fill each cone with 2½ tablespoons batter. Bake 30 minutes or until cake tops spring back when lightly touched and toothpick inserted into centers comes out clean. Remove cones to wire rack; cool completely.

3. Cut pointy flames from fruit rolls using kitchen shears or sharp knife. Fold or roll flames so they stand upright on their own. Blend food coloring into frosting, a few drops at a time, until desired shade of yellow is reached. Frost cupcake tops. Place flames on cupcakes before frosting sets.

BIG CHEEK BUNNY CAKE

Makes 12 servings

1 package (18¼ ounces) cake mix, any flavor, plus ingredients
    to prepare mix
Fluffy White Frosting (recipe follows)
1 (15×10-inch) cake board or large tray, covered
2 cups shredded coconut, tinted pink*
2 purchased coconut-covered cupcakes
Red string licorice
Assorted candies

To tint coconut, dilute a few drops of red food coloring with ½ teaspoon water in a large resealable food storage bag; add coconut. Seal the bag and shake well until evenly coated. If a deeper color is desired, add more diluted food coloring and shake again.

1. Preheat oven to 350°F. Prepare and bake cake mix in two 8- or 9-inch round cake pans according to package directions. Cool in pans on wire racks 10 minutes. Remove from pans to racks; cool completely.

2. Prepare Fluffy White Frosting. Cut out cake pieces from 1 cake round as shown in diagram 1 (page 105). Position cakes on prepared cake board as shown in diagram 2, connecting pieces with small amount of frosting. Frost cake with remaining frosting; sprinkle with coconut. Decorate with cupcakes, licorice and candies as desired.

FLUFFY WHITE FROSTING: Combine 1 container (16 ounces) vanilla frosting and ¾ cup marshmallow creme in medium bowl; mix well. Makes about 2 cups.

1.

B · 1" · B

A

├── 4" ──┤

2.

B B

A

BOO HANDS CUPCAKES

Makes 24 cupcakes

 1 package (18¼ ounces) cake mix, any flavor, plus
       ingredients to prepare mix
 1 container (16 ounces) white frosting
36 large marshmallows
24 black jelly beans, halved
12 orange jelly beans, halved

1. Preheat oven to 350°F. Line 24 standard (2½-inch) muffin cups with paper baking cups.

2. Prepare cake mix according to package directions. Spoon batter evenly into prepared muffin cups. Bake according to package directions. Cool cupcakes in pans on wire racks 15 minutes. Remove to racks; cool completely.

3. Spread small amount of frosting on cupcakes. Cut marshmallows in half crosswise; place one half on each cupcake. Frost cupcakes again, completely covering marshmallow halves.

4. Roll remaining marshmallows between hands until they are about 2½ inches long. Cut in half and arrange on either side of cupcakes to create hands; cover completely with frosting.

5. Create faces using 2 black jelly bean halves for eyes and orange jelly bean half for nose. Swirl frosting on top of ghosts as shown in photo.

JACK IN THE BOX

Makes 8 servings

(*pictured on page 55*)

1 package (18¼ ounces) cake mix, any flavor, plus
  ingredients to prepare mix
1 scoop ice cream or coconut-covered cupcake
  Assorted candies
1 container (16 ounces) white frosting
  Assorted food colorings
  Flat red candy strips or chewy fruit rolls
1 sugar ice cream cone

1. Preheat oven to 350°F. Prepare and bake cake mix according to package directions for two 8- or 9-inch square cakes. Cool completely.

2. Place ice cream in small dish. Decorate with assorted candies to create face. Place in freezer until ready to serve.

3. Blend frosting and food colorings until desired shades are reached. Cut one cake layer into 4 equal pieces. (Reserve remaining cake layer for snacking or discard.) Place each piece one at a time on serving plate, spreading frosting between each layer. Frost top and sides of cake.

4. Press assorted candies around top, base and edges of cake. Create clown collar by pinching candy strips into 4-inch circle; place on center of cake. Decorate ice cream cone, if desired. To serve, place ice cream face on top of candy collar; top with ice cream cone. Serve immediately.

Super Snacks

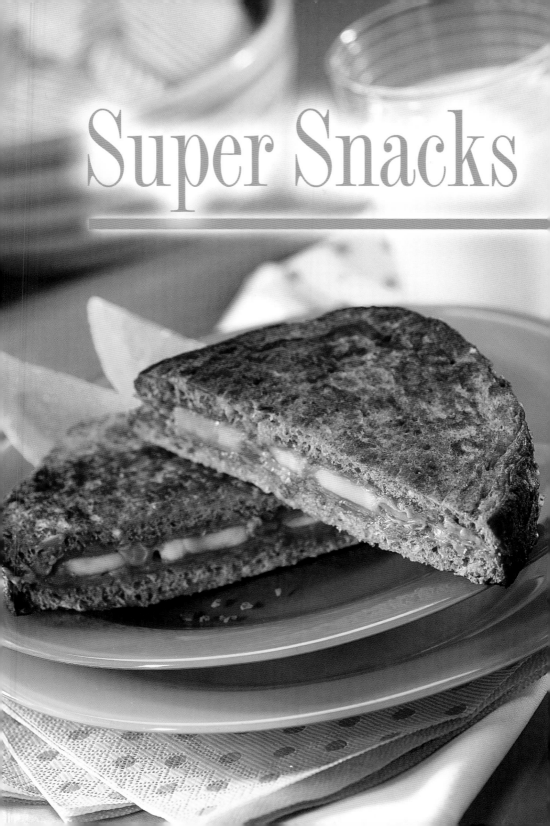

TABLE OF CONTENTS

AT THE ZOO   112

OUT OF THIS WORLD   126

SUMMER VACATION   144

INDEX   156

AT THE ZOO

FROZEN FLORIDA MONKEY MALTS

Makes 2 servings

2 bananas, peeled
1 cup milk
5 tablespoons frozen orange juice concentrate
3 tablespoons malted milk powder

1. Wrap bananas in plastic wrap; freeze.

2. Break bananas into pieces; place in blender with milk, orange juice concentrate and malted milk powder. Blend until smooth; pour into glasses to serve.

ZEBRAS

Makes about 3 dozen cookies

  2 **packages (18 ounces each) refrigerated sugar cookie dough**
$\frac{1}{2}$ **cup all-purpose flour**
$\frac{1}{2}$ **cup unsweetened Dutch process cocoa powder***
   Prepared dark chocolate frosting
   Chocolate sprinkles
   Mini chocolate chips and regular chocolate chips

*Dutch process or European-style cocoa gives the cookies an intense chocolate flavor and a dark, rich color. Other unsweetened cocoas can be substituted, but the flavor may be milder and the color lighter.

1. Let both packages of dough stand at room temperature about 15 minutes.

2. Combine 1 package of dough and flour in large bowl; beat until well blended. Combine remaining package of dough and cocoa in another large bowl; beat until well blended. Wrap doughs separately in plastic wrap; freeze 15 minutes.

3. Roll out each flavor of dough separately into 9-inch square between lightly floured pieces of waxed paper. Remove waxed paper. Place cocoa dough on top of plain dough. Cut into four 4½-inch squares. Layer squares on top of each other, alternating cocoa and plain doughs, to make 1 stack. Wrap in plastic wrap; refrigerate at least 4 hours or up to 2 days.

4. Preheat oven to 350°F. Lightly grease cookie sheets. Trim edges of dough square if necessary. Cut dough into ¼-inch striped slices, wiping off knife after each cut; cut slices in half into 2¼×2-inch rectangles. Place rectangles 2 inches apart on prepared cookie sheets.

5. Work with stripes vertically. For each zebra, cut small triangle from top left corner and narrow triangle from top right edge (diagram 1, page 115). (Reserve scraps for snacking or discard.) Cut small triangle from center of bottom edge; place at top of cookie for ear (diagram 2).

6. Bake 10 minutes or until edges are light brown. Cool cookies on cookie sheets 5 minutes. Remove to wire racks; cool completely.

7. For manes, spread frosting on cookie edges at both sides of ear; top with sprinkles. Attach 1 mini chocolate chip for eye and 1 regular chocolate chip for nostril on each cookie with frosting as shown in photo.

about 2"

about 2-1/4"

Diagram 1

Diagram 2

CHOCOLATE BEARS

Makes 16 (4-inch) cookies

1 recipe Chocolate Cookie Dough (page 14)
  White and colored frostings
  Decorating gels
  Coarse sugars
  Assorted small candies

1. Prepare Chocolate Cookie Dough.

2. Preheat oven to 325°F. Grease cookie sheets. Divide dough in half. Refrigerate one half of dough.

3. Divide remaining dough into 8 equal balls. Cut 1 dough ball in half; roll 1 half into ball for body. Cut other half into 2 equal pieces; roll 1 piece into 4 small dough balls for paws. Divide second piece into thirds. Roll two-thirds of dough into ball for head. Divide remaining one-third of dough in half; roll into 2 small dough balls for ears.

4. Assemble balls to form bear shape on prepared cookie sheet. Repeat with remaining dough balls and dough from refrigerator.

5. Bake 13 to 15 minutes or until set. Cool completely on cookie sheets. Decorate with frostings, gels, sugars and candies as desired.

To get
bright colors and to
keep the frostings at the proper
consistency, tint them with paste
food colors.

LUSCIOUS LIONS & LIONESS COOKIES

Makes about 4 dozen cookies

MANES

    1 package (about 16 ounces) refrigerated sugar cookie dough
    ¼ cup all-purpose flour
    2 tablespoons powdered sugar
      Grated peel of 1 large orange
    ¼ teaspoon yellow gel food coloring
    ¼ teaspoon red gel food coloring

FACES

    1 package (about 16 ounces) refrigerated sugar cookie dough
    ¼ cup all-purpose flour
    2 tablespoons powdered sugar
      Grated peel of 2 lemons
    ½ teaspoon yellow gel food coloring
      Mini candy-coated chocolate pieces
      Prepared white icing and assorted decors
      Prepared chocolate icing or melted chocolate

1. Generously grease 2 cookie sheets. For manes, remove 1 package of dough from wrapper; place in large bowl. Let dough stand at room temperature about 15 minutes.

2. Add ¼ cup flour, 2 tablespoons powdered sugar, orange peel, ¼ teaspoon yellow food coloring and red food coloring to dough; beat with electric mixer at medium speed until well blended and evenly colored. Shape into 24 large balls. Place 12 balls on each cookie sheet. Flatten balls into circles about 2¾ inches in diameter. Cut each circle with fluted 2½-inch round cookie cutter. Remove and discard scraps. Refrigerate 30 minutes.

3. Preheat oven to 350°F. Bake 12 to 14 minutes or until lightly browned. Remove from oven. Cool on cookie sheets 2 to 3 minutes. Remove to wire racks; cool completely.

4. For faces, remove remaining package of dough from wrapper; place in medium bowl. Let dough stand at room temperature about 15 minutes.

5. Add ¼ cup flour, 2 tablespoons powdered sugar, lemon peel and ½ teaspoon yellow food coloring to dough; beat with electric mixer at medium speed until well blended and evenly colored. Shape into 48 balls. Place on prepared cookie sheets. Flatten balls to slightly larger than 1½ inches in diameter. Cut into circles using smooth 1½-inch round cookie cutter. Remove dough scraps; shape into ears. Attach 2 ears to each face. Place 2 candy pieces in center of each ear and place 1 candy piece for nose.

6. Bake 14 minutes or until lightly browned. Cool on cookie sheets 2 to 3 minutes. Remove to wire racks; cool completely.

7. To assemble lions attach 24 lion faces to manes with icing. Leave remaining faces plain for lioness cookies. Pipe white icing onto faces and press decors into icing for eyes. Pipe chocolate icing onto faces for whiskers.

SNAKE STROMBOLI

Makes 24 to 48 servings

  2 loaves (16 ounces each) frozen white bread dough, thawed
  4 tablespoons mustard, divided
  2 tablespoons sun-dried tomato pesto, divided
  2 teaspoons Italian seasoning, divided
10 ounces thinly sliced ham, divided
10 ounces thinly sliced salami, divided
1½ cups (6 ounces) shredded provolone cheese, divided
1½ cups (6 ounces) shredded mozzarella cheese, divided
  3 egg yolks
  3 teaspoons water
    Red, yellow and green liquid food colorings
    Sliced green olives and red bell pepper strips

1. Line 2 baking sheets with parchment paper; spray with nonstick cooking spray. Roll out 1 loaf of dough on lightly floured work surface into 24×6-inch rectangle. Spread 2 tablespoons mustard and 1 tablespoon pesto over dough, leaving 1-inch border; sprinkle with 1 teaspoon Italian seasoning.

2. Layer half of ham and salami over dough. Sprinkle ¾ cup of each cheese over meats. Brush edges of dough with water. Beginning at long side, tightly roll up dough. Pinch all edges to seal. Transfer roll to prepared cookie sheet, seam side down, and shape into S-shaped snake or coiled snake (leave one end unattached to form head on coil). Repeat with remaining ingredients.

3. Combine 1 egg yolk, 1 teaspoon water and red food coloring in small bowl; 1 egg yolk, 1 teaspoon water and yellow food coloring in separate small bowl; 1 egg yolk with remaining teaspoon water and green food coloring in additional small bowl. Paint stripes, dots and zigzags over dough to make snakeskin pattern.

4. Let dough rise, uncovered, in warm place 30 minutes, or 40 minutes if using coil shape. Taper ends of dough to form head. Shape and score tail end to form rattle, if desired. Preheat oven to 375°F.

5. Bake 25 to 30 minutes. Cool slightly. Use olives for eyes and pepper strips for tongues. Slice and serve warm.

CHOO-CHOO TRAIN

Makes 1 (4-car) train cookie

1 package (18 ounces) refrigerated cookie dough, any flavor
All-purpose flour (optional)
Blue Cookie Glaze (recipe follows)
Assorted colored icings, colored candies, small decors
2 small peanut butter sandwich crackers

1. Draw patterns for 4 train cars on cardboard using diagrams below; cut out patterns. Preheat oven to 350°F. Line cookie sheet with parchment paper.

2. Remove dough from wrapper. Roll out dough on lightly floured surface to 18×13-inch rectangle. Sprinkle with flour to minimize sticking, if necessary. Place on prepared cookie sheet.

3. Bake 8 to 10 minutes or until lightly browned. Cool on cookie sheet 5 minutes. Slide cookie and parchment paper onto wire rack; cool 5 minutes.

4. Lay sheet of waxed paper over cookie while still warm. Place patterns over waxed paper. Cut cookie around patterns with sharp knife; remove patterns and waxed paper. Cover with towel; cool completely.

5. Spread Blue Cookie Glaze on train cars as shown in photo. Allow glaze to set about 30 minutes before decorating. Decorate with icings, candies and decors as shown in photo. Use peanut butter sandwich crackers as large train wheels.

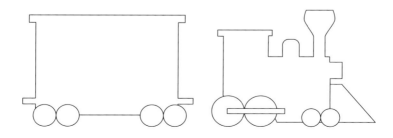

BLUE COOKIE GLAZE

Makes 1 cup

2 cups powdered sugar
7 to 9 tablespoons heavy cream, divided
  Blue food coloring

Combine powdered sugar and 6 tablespoons cream in medium bowl; whisk until smooth. Add enough remaining cream, 1 tablespoon at a time, to make a medium-thick pourable glaze. Tint glaze with food coloring, a few drops at a time, until desired shade of blue is reached.

FISH BAIT WITH GATOR HEADS

Makes 6 servings

6 ounces assorted frozen clam strips, breaded fish pieces or breaded shrimp
3 to 5 drops green food coloring
1 cup tartar sauce
6 (6-inch) bamboo skewers
6 dill pickles
6 to 8 pimiento-stuffed green olives
2 pepperoni pieces, cut into 3 strips each
  Mustard

1. Bake seafood pieces according to package directions.

2. Meanwhile, stir food coloring into tartar sauce in small serving bowl until desired shade of green is reached; set aside.

3. Thread 3 or 4 seafood pieces onto each skewer when cool enough to handle. Place on serving platter and keep warm.

4. Cut horizontal slit in each pickle for alligator's mouth. Insert strip of pepperoni to make tongue. Slice olives to make eyes and nostrils; attach to pickle with mustard. Arrange alligators around fish skewers and serve with tartar sauce.

Out of this World

CHERRY TOMATO PLANETS

Makes about 20 appetizers

1 bag (20 ounces) cherry tomatoes
¼ cup (1 ounce) shredded mozzarella cheese
20 slices pepperoni

1. Preheat broiler. Slice top ⅛ inch off stem end of tomatoes using paring knife, keeping top and bottom pieces next to each other. Seed and core tomatoes using small melon baller or by carefully pinching out core using thumb and index finger.

2. Fill each tomato with cheese; top with slice of pepperoni and cover with tomato top. Secure with toothpick.

3. Place filled tomatoes on baking sheet and broil on top oven rack, about 6 inches from heat source, 3 minutes, until cheese is melted and tomatoes just begin to shrivel.

4. Transfer tomatoes to paper towel-lined plate to drain. Remove toothpicks before serving. Serve warm.

MOON ROCKS

Makes 3 dozen cookies

1 package (18 ounces) refrigerated sugar cookie dough
1 cup uncooked quick oats
¾ cup butterscotch chips
¾ cup yogurt-covered raisins

1. Preheat oven to 350°F. Lightly grease cookie sheets. Let dough stand at room temperature about 15 minutes.

2. Combine dough, oats, butterscotch chips and raisins in large bowl; beat with electric mixer at medium speed until well blended. Drop dough by rounded teaspoonfuls 2 inches apart onto prepared cookie sheets.

3. Bake 9 to 11 minutes or until set. Cool on cookie sheets 1 minute. Remove to wire racks; cool completely.

Quick oats and old-fashioned oats are essentially the same. The quick oats cook faster because they have been rolled into thinner flakes.

Moon Rocks

PHASES-OF-THE-MOON TOASTED CHEESE

Makes 36 servings

36 slices white bread (about 2 loaves)
36 slices white American cheese
18 slices yellow American cheese

1. Remove top oven rack. Preheat broiler. Line oven rack with foil. Place bread slices in single layer on prepared rack. Replace rack; broil 1 minute or until bread is toasted; flip and broil about 20 seconds more. Remove and repeat with remaining bread slices. *Reduce oven temperature to 225°F.*

2. Top each toast slice with 1 slice white cheese. Cut 4 rounds out of each cheese-covered toast with 1½-inch round cookie cutter; discard scraps.

3. Cut 4 rounds out of each slice of yellow cheese using same cookie cutter. Cut rounds into shapes to resemble eight phases of moon (crescents, halves, three-quarters and full moon). Place shapes on top of toasted white cheese rounds. (Leave some plain to represent new moon.)

4. Place rounds on baking sheet; bake 10 minutes or just until cheese is melted.

CRUNCHY COMETS

Makes 12 to 14 servings

1 package (8 ounces) cream cheese, softened
⅓ cup granulated sugar
1 egg yolk
1 tablespoon all-purpose flour
1 teaspoon vanilla
½ teaspoon almond extract
1 package (16 ounces) phyllo dough, thawed
1 cup (2 sticks) butter, melted and cooled
1 can (21 ounces) cherry pie filling
   Powdered sugar
   Red decorating sugar

1. Preheat oven to 375°F. Whisk cream cheese, granulated sugar, egg yolk, flour, vanilla and almond extracts in medium bowl until smooth. Chill filling 10 to 15 minutes.

2. Unroll thawed phyllo dough on sheet of waxed paper. Lift off one sheet onto work surface and cover remaining dough with sheets of waxed paper and clean, damp towel to keep moist. Brush single sheet of phyllo with thin layer of melted butter. Fold buttered dough in half, brushing edges with additional butter as needed. Dot 1 tablespoon cream cheese filling 3 inches away from corner of rectangle. Top with 1 or 2 cherries from pie filling. Turn exposed corner of dough up over filling and fold in sides to secure. Roll and twist dough into tail shape. Repeat with remaining dough and filling. Reserve extra pie filling.

3. Make 3-inch thick roll of crumpled aluminum foil; place lengthwise on baking sheet. Carefully lay twisted ends of phyllo over foil, bending slightly to form curved comet tails. Brush with melted butter and bake 12 to 15 minutes or until golden brown. Dust with powdered sugar and red sugar. Serve comets with reserved cherry pie filling on the side.

TIP: Comets may be baked ahead of time and chilled without decorations. Warm in oven to restore crispness before sprinkling with colored sugar.

GALAXY GEL

Makes 16 servings

4 packages (3 ounces each) gelatin (yellow, orange, red and blue)
4 cups boiling water
4 cups ice cold water
¼ cantaloupe, seeded
¼ seedless watermelon
2 large apples, peeled

1. Pour each flavor of gelatin into separate medium bowl. Add 1 cup boiling water to each. Stir 2 minutes to dissolve completely. Add 1 cup cold water to each bowl. Refrigerate 20 to 25 minutes until slightly thickened.

2. Scoop out round planets from cantaloupe and watermelon using both ends of melon ball tool. Cut apples into ⅓-inch-thick slices. Use small star cookie cutter or small knife to cut into stars.

3. Lightly spray 2-quart glass bowl with nonstick cooking spray. Pour thickened yellow gelatin on bottom. Arrange 4 to 5 pieces of fruit on top of gelatin near sides; chill 5 minutes. Carefully pour orange gelatin over yellow gelatin and fruit. Place additional fruit on top of second layer and chill 5 minutes. Repeat with red gelatin and remaining fruit. Finish with blue gelatin; cover and chill in refrigerator 4 hours or more. Unmold onto platter or serve directly from bowl.

Unmold gelatin by pulling it away from bowl edges with moistened fingertips. Dip bowl, almost to rim, in warm water for 10 seconds. Cover bowl with serving plate, invert and shake lose.

SPACE SHUTTLES

Makes 6 servings

6 small bananas
2 packages (12 ounces each) white chocolate chips
3 to 4 tablespoons vegetable shortening
9 mini oval sandwich cookies or vanilla wafers, cut in half
1 bag (6 ounces) black licorice bits
1 bag (14 ounces) red licorice strings, cut into 2-inch pieces
1 tube black decorating gel

1. Peel and trim ends of bananas to make shuttle shapes. Freeze bananas 15 minutes.

2. Melt white chocolate chips and shortening in microwavable bowl. Stir until mixture is smooth and pourable; cool slightly.

3. Remove bananas from freezer. Place 6 forks in 13×9-inch baking pan; arrange bananas on forks in pan, making sure bananas do not touch bottom of pan. Slowly spoon melted white chocolate over bananas, covering completely. Let stand until set. Turn bananas and repeat on other side. Place bananas on parchment-lined baking sheets. Refrigerate coated bananas until white chocolate is firm.

4. Dip cookie slices into melted white chocolate, coating evenly on both sides. Press 3 cookie slices into each shuttle to create flanges at base. Refrigerate until firm.

5. Attach 3 or 4 black licorice bits using melted white chocolate to bottom of each shuttle; insert red licorice strands in center. Decorate with black decorating gel. Refrigerate until ready to serve.

TIP: Make your shuttles soar through the sky! Serve them on blue plates resting on a cloud of flaked coconut.

EARTH'S CORE MEATBALLS

Makes 12 servings

25 medium to large cherry tomatoes, halved and seeded
3 to 4 ounces mozzarella cheese, cut into ¼- to ½-inch cubes
2 eggs, divided
2 pounds ground beef
1½ cups Italian-style bread crumbs, divided
1 teaspoon salt
¾ teaspoon garlic powder
½ teaspoon black pepper
   Hot cooked pasta (optional)
   Prepared pasta sauce, heated (optional)

1. Preheat oven to 350°F. Line two baking sheets with foil and spray generously with nonstick cooking spray; set aside.

2. Insert 1 cheese cube into one tomato half; cover with another half to encase cheese.

3. Lightly beat one egg in large bowl. Add beef, ½ cup bread crumbs, salt, garlic powder and pepper; stir until well mixed. Shape 2 tablespoons beef mixture into rough 2-inch circle. Place cheese-filled tomato in center; bring edges of circle together to completely encase tomato. Lightly roll meatball to form smooth ball. Place on prepared baking sheet. Repeat with remaining meat mixture, tomatoes and cheese.

4. Lightly beat remaining egg in medium shallow bowl. Place 1 cup bread crumbs in another shallow bowl. Dip meatballs one at a time into beaten egg, shake off excess and roll in bread crumbs. Return to baking sheet. Bake 35 minutes until meatballs are slightly crisp and are no longer pink, turning meatballs halfway through baking time. Serve on pasta with sauce, if desired.

SPACE DUST BARS

Makes 1½ dozen bars

1 package (12 ounces) white chocolate chips
⅓ cup butter
2 cups graham cracker crumbs
1 cup chopped pecans
2 cans (12 ounces each) apricot pastry filling
1 cup sweetened flaked coconut
   Additional sweetened flaked coconut (optional)
   Powdered sugar (optional)

1. Preheat oven to 350°F. Grease 13×9-inch baking pan. Combine white chocolate chips and butter in medium saucepan; cook and stir over low heat until melted and smooth. Remove from heat; stir in graham cracker crumbs and pecans. Let cool 5 minutes.

2. Press half of crumb mixture onto bottom of prepared pan. Bake 10 minutes or until golden brown. Remove from oven; spread apricot filling evenly over crust. Combine coconut with remaining crumb mixture; sprinkle evenly over apricot filling.

3. Bake 20 to 25 minutes or until light golden brown. Cool completely in pan on wire rack. Sprinkle with additional coconut and powdered sugar, if desired. Cut into bars.

TIP: For place cards, cut Space Dust Bars into circles and put one at each place setting. In the center of each circle, add a small plastic astronaut figure holding a paper flag with the guest's name on it.

FLYING SAUCER ICE CREAM SANDWICHES

Makes 22 servings

   3 cups vanilla ice cream
   1 package (9 ounces) chocolate wafer cookies
22 mini chocolate-covered peppermint patties
   Chocolate-covered candies

1. Let ice cream stand at room temperature about 10 minutes to soften slightly. Line baking sheet with waxed paper or foil; place in freezer.

2. Scoop 2 tablespoons ice cream onto one chocolate wafer. Top with second wafer; press wafers together slightly to push ice cream to edges, scraping any excess from edges. Place on prepared baking sheet in freezer. Repeat with remaining ingredients. Leave sandwiches in freezer until frozen solid.

3. Decorate sandwiches one at a time. To attach chocolate peppermint patties to tops of each sandwich, heat table knife over stove burner for a few seconds or until hot. Rub knife on candy until it begins to melt and get sticky. Lightly press candy melted side down to center top of one sandwich. Hold until secure. Reheat knife; melt small area on top of chocolate candy. Stick chocolate-covered candy to melted area and hold until secure. Decorate ice cream edges of sandwich with more chocolate-covered candies. Return to freezer. Repeat with remaining sandwiches.

4. Keep frozen until ready to serve.

SUMMER VACATION

SALMON CELERY TREES

Makes 12 servings

1 can (6 ounces) boneless skinless pink salmon
2 tablespoons minced fresh dill
1 tablespoon minced green onion
1 tablespoon lemon juice
6 ounces cream cheese, softened
   Salt and black pepper
12 celery stalks
   Fresh dill sprigs, 3 to 4 inches long

1. Combine salmon, dill, green onion and lemon juice in medium bowl until well blended. Add cream cheese and mash with fork until mixture is smooth. Season to taste with salt and pepper.

2. Stack celery stalks in pairs. Cut each pair into 3-inch pieces.

3. Spread 2 tablespoons salmon mixture into hollowed section of each celery piece with small spoon or knife. Press dill sprigs into one half of each celery pair before pressing filled sides together. Place upright on serving platter with dill sprigs on top to resemble trees.

CONCH SHELLS

Makes 24 servings

2 tablespoons butter, softened
2 tablespoons packed brown sugar
⅛ teaspoon ground cinnamon
1 can (8 ounces) refrigerated crescent roll dough
½ cup raisins
1 egg white, slightly beaten
    Granulated sugar

1. Preheat oven to 350°F. Combine butter, brown sugar and cinnamon in small bowl; set aside.

2. Unroll crescent roll dough and separate into pre-scored triangles. Cut each triangle into 3 equal size triangles. Spread 1 side of each triangle with about ½ teaspoon butter mixture; sprinkle evenly with raisins. Roll each triangle at a slight angle from the straight-sided base toward the triangular tip in the shape of a conch shell. Place on baking sheet.

3. Brush rolls with egg white and sprinkle with granulated sugar. Bake 8 to 10 minutes or until golden brown. Cool on wire rack.

SERVING SUGGESTION: Design your own sea shore! Make sand by combining equal parts finely crushed graham crackers and raw sugar crystals. Spread sand on a large platter and arrange conch shells on top.

APPLE-CHEDDAR PANINI

Makes 4 sandwiches

(pictured on back cover)

1 tablespoon butter
2 cups thinly sliced apples*
¼ teaspoon ground cinnamon
8 teaspoons apple jelly
8 slices egg bread
4 slices (1 ounce each) mild Cheddar cheese

*Use sweet apples such as Royal Gala or Fuji.

1. Melt butter in large nonstick skillet. Add apple slices; sprinkle with cinnamon. Cook and stir over medium heat 5 minutes or until golden and tender. Remove from skillet; wipe out skillet with paper towel.

2. Spread 2 teaspoons apple jelly on each of 4 bread slices; top with 1 cheese slice. Arrange one fourth of apple slices over each cheese slice. Top with remaining 4 bread slices.

3. Heat same skillet over medium heat until hot. Add sandwiches; press down lightly with spatula or weigh down with small plate. Cook sandwiches 4 to 5 minutes per side or until cheese melts and sandwiches are golden brown.

The peak season for U.S. grown apples is September through November. Royal Gala apples, which are imported from Australia and New Zealand, are at their peak from April through July.

SUPER PEANUT BUTTER SANDWICHES

Makes 4 servings

(pictured on tab)

⅔ cup peanut butter
2 tablespoons toasted wheat germ
1 tablespoon honey
8 slices firm whole wheat or multi-grain bread
1 ripe banana, sliced
2 eggs, beaten
⅓ cup orange juice
1 tablespoon grated orange peel
1 tablespoon butter or margarine

1. Combine peanut butter, wheat germ and honey in small bowl. Spread evenly on one side of each bread slice.

2. Place banana slices on top of peanut butter mixture on four slices of bread. Top with remaining bread slices, peanut butter side down. Lightly press together.

3. Combine eggs, orange juice and orange peel in shallow dish. Dip sandwiches in egg mixture, coating both sides.

4. Melt butter in large skillet. Cook sandwiches over medium heat until golden brown, turning once. Serve immediately.

Prep Time: 15 minutes

FRENCH FRIED CACTI

Makes 24 servings

4 cups chicken or vegetable broth
2 cups medium-grain rice
1½ teaspoons salt
2 cups grated Parmesan cheese
1½ cups (6 ounces) shredded mozzarella cheese
3 eggs, lightly beaten
Green gel food coloring
2 cups panko*
2 cups vegetable oil for frying

Panko bread crumbs are light, crispy, Japanese-style bread crumbs. They can be found in the Asian aisle of most supermarkets. Unseasoned dry bread crumbs can be substituted.

1. Combine broth, rice and salt in large saucepan. Bring to a boil; reduce heat to simmer and partially cover. Simmer, stirring occasionally, 15 to 20 minutes or until rice is tender and liquid is absorbed.

2. Remove rice from heat; mix in cheeses until melted. Beat in eggs rapidly. Add food coloring until mixture is pale green. Chill 8 hours or overnight.

3. Line 3 baking sheets with waxed paper. Place bread crumbs on plate. Roll 2 tablespoons rice mixture between hands into 3½-inch log. Roll 2 teaspoons mixture into 2-inch log; attach smaller log to larger log to make branch. Gently dredge rice cactus in crumbs; place on prepared baking sheet. Repeat with remaining rice mixture. Refrigerate about 30 minutes.

4. Line platter with paper towels. Heat vegetable oil to 360°F in medium heavy skillet. Fry 3 or 4 cacti at a time, turning once, about 4 minutes or until golden brown; remove to prepared platter. Sprinkle with salt.

TIP: Serve with a dipping sauce of your choice, such as salsa, warmed marinara sauce or honey mustard.

WACKY WATERMELON

Makes 12 servings

4 cups diced seedless watermelon (1-inch cubes)
¼ cup strawberry fruit spread
2 cups vanilla frozen yogurt
2 tablespoons mini chocolate chips, divided

1. Place 2 cups watermelon and fruit spread in blender. Cover and pulse on low until smooth. Repeat with remaining watermelon. Add yogurt, 1 cup at a time, pulsing until smooth after each addition.

2. Pour mixture into 8×4-inch loaf pan. Freeze 2 hours or until mixture begins to harden around edge of pan. Stir well until mixture is smooth and slushy. Stir in 1½ tablespoons chocolate chips. Smooth mixture with back of spoon. Sprinkle evenly with remaining chocolate chips. Cover pan with foil; freeze 6 hours or overnight.

3. To serve, place pan in warm water briefly; invert onto cutting board. Let stand 5 minutes on cutting board to soften slightly. Cut loaf into slices. Serve immediately.

4. Wrap leftover slices individually in plastic wrap and place upright in clean loaf pan. Store in freezer.

SLAM DUNK

Makes 12 servings

(pictured on back cover)

1 package (18¼ ounces) dark chocolate cake mix, plus ingredients
    to prepare mix
¾ cup crushed chocolate sandwich cookies (about 8 to 10)
1 container (16 ounces) dark chocolate frosting
1 cup prepared vanilla frosting
  Round hard sweet and sour candies
  Red, yellow and blue food coloring
  Brown mini candy-coated chocolate pieces
  Assorted candy-coated chocolate pieces (optional)

1. Prepare and bake cake mix in two 9-inch round cake pans according to package directions. Cool completely on wire racks.

2. Place one cake layer on serving plate; spread with chocolate frosting. Sprinkle crushed cookie crumbs over frosting. Top with second cake layer. Frost side of cake with chocolate frosting, being careful not to get frosting on top of cake.

3. Blend vanilla frosting and several drops of red, yellow and blue food coloring in small bowl until desired shade of orange is reached. Spread over top of cake. Gently press meat mallet into frosting to create texture of basketball. Arrange mini chocolate pieces on cake as shown on back cover. Press chocolate pieces around bottom of cake, if desired.

FROZEN PUDDING CUPS

Makes 8 servings

(pictured on front cover)

1 package (4-serving size) chocolate instant pudding mix
5 cups cold milk, divided
1 package (4-serving size) vanilla instant pudding mix
   Fresh sliced strawberries

1. Whisk together chocolate pudding mix and 2½ cups milk in medium bowl about 2 minutes. Repeat with vanilla pudding mix and remaining 2½ cups milk in another medium bowl.

2. Divide half of chocolate pudding among 8 plastic cups. Layer half of vanilla pudding over chocolate pudding in cups. Repeat layers; cover with plastic wrap and freeze until firm, about 3 hours. Thaw pudding cups at room temperature 1 hour before serving. Top with sliced strawberries.

POTATO BUGS

Makes about 15 servings

1 package (16 ounces) shredded potato nuggets
6 pieces uncooked spaghetti, broken into thirds
1 carrot, cut into matchstick-size strips
   Sour cream, black olive slices, ketchup and broccoli pieces

1. Preheat oven to 450°F. Lightly grease baking sheets.

2. Spread potato nuggets on baking sheets. Bake 7 minutes. Loosen nuggets from baking sheets with metal spatula.

3. Thread 3 potato nuggets onto 1 spaghetti piece. Bake 5 minutes.

4. Carefully push carrot strips into sides of nuggets for legs. Attach vegetables with sour cream to create faces as desired.

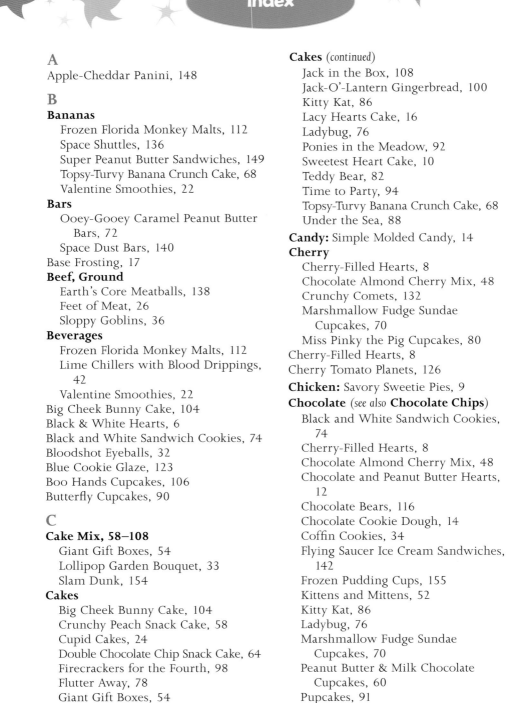

Index

A

Apple-Cheddar Panini, 148

B

Bananas
Frozen Florida Monkey Malts, 112
Space Shuttles, 136
Super Peanut Butter Sandwiches, 149
Topsy-Turvy Banana Crunch Cake, 68
Valentine Smoothies, 22
Bars
Ooey-Gooey Caramel Peanut Butter
Bars, 72
Space Dust Bars, 140
Base Frosting, 17
Beef, Ground
Earth's Core Meatballs, 138
Feet of Meat, 26
Sloppy Goblins, 36
Beverages
Frozen Florida Monkey Malts, 112
Lime Chillers with Blood Drippings,
42
Valentine Smoothies, 22
Big Cheek Bunny Cake, 104
Black & White Hearts, 6
Black and White Sandwich Cookies, 74
Bloodshot Eyeballs, 32
Blue Cookie Glaze, 123
Boo Hands Cupcakes, 106
Butterfly Cupcakes, 90

C

Cake Mix, 58–108
Giant Gift Boxes, 54
Lollipop Garden Bouquet, 33
Slam Dunk, 154
Cakes
Big Cheek Bunny Cake, 104
Crunchy Peach Snack Cake, 58
Cupid Cakes, 24
Double Chocolate Chip Snack Cake, 64
Firecrackers for the Fourth, 98
Flutter Away, 78
Giant Gift Boxes, 54

Cakes (continued)
Jack in the Box, 108
Jack-O'-Lantern Gingerbread, 100
Kitty Kat, 86
Lacy Hearts Cake, 16
Ladybug, 76
Ponies in the Meadow, 92
Sweetest Heart Cake, 10
Teddy Bear, 82
Time to Party, 94
Topsy-Turvy Banana Crunch Cake, 68
Under the Sea, 88
Candy: Simple Molded Candy, 14
Cherry
Cherry-Filled Hearts, 8
Chocolate Almond Cherry Mix, 48
Crunchy Comets, 132
Marshmallow Fudge Sundae
Cupcakes, 70
Miss Pinky the Pig Cupcakes, 80
Cherry-Filled Hearts, 8
Cherry Tomato Planets, 126
Chicken: Savory Sweetie Pies, 9
Chocolate (see also **Chocolate Chips**)
Black and White Sandwich Cookies,
74
Cherry-Filled Hearts, 8
Chocolate Almond Cherry Mix, 48
Chocolate and Peanut Butter Hearts,
12
Chocolate Bears, 116
Chocolate Cookie Dough, 14
Coffin Cookies, 34
Flying Saucer Ice Cream Sandwiches,
142
Frozen Pudding Cups, 155
Kittens and Mittens, 52
Kitty Kat, 86
Ladybug, 76
Marshmallow Fudge Sundae
Cupcakes, 70
Peanut Butter & Milk Chocolate
Cupcakes, 60
Pupcakes, 91

Chocolate (continued)
Slam Dunk, 154
Spider Cakes, 38
Sweet Mysteries, 62
Teddy Bear, 82
Time to Party, 94
Under the Sea, 88
Zebras, 114
Chocolate Almond Cherry Mix, 48
Chocolate and Peanut Butter Hearts, 12
Chocolate Bears, 116
Chocolate Chips
Black & White Hearts, 6
Chocolate-Dipped Strawberries, 20
Double Chocolate Chip Snack Cake,
64
Ooey-Gooey Caramel Peanut Butter
Bars, 72
Space Dust Bars, 140
Space Shuttles, 136
Teddy Bear, 82
Wacky Watermelon, 152
Chocolate Cookie Dough, 14
Chocolate-Dipped Strawberries, 20
Choo-Choo Train, 122
Christmas Tree Rolls, 50
Cinnamon Cereal Crispies, 65
Coconut
Big Cheek Bunny Cake, 104
Ladybug, 76
Ponies in the Meadow, 92
Space Dust Bars, 140
Sweetest Heart Cake, 10
Coffin Cookies, 34
Conch Shells, 146
Cookies
Black & White Hearts, 6
Black and White Sandwich Cookies,
74
Bloodshot Eyeballs, 32
Chocolate and Peanut Butter Hearts,
12
Chocolate Bears, 116
Choo-Choo Train, 122

Cookies (continued)
Cinnamon Cereal Crispies, 65
Coffin Cookies, 34
Ice Cream Sandwich Hearts, 4
Kittens and Mittens, 52
Meringue Bone Cookies, 28
Moon Rocks, 128
Skeleton Cookies, 44
Snowball Bites, 46
Strawberry Hearts, 18
Sunshine Sandwiches, 66
Sweet Mysteries, 62
Zebras, 114
Creamy White Frosting, 17
Creepy Cobwebs, 40
Crunchy Comets, 132
Crunchy Peach Snack Cake, 58
Cupcakes
Boo Hands Cupcakes, 106
Butterfly Cupcakes, 90
Doodle Bug Cupcakes, 84
Liberty's Torches, 102
Luck o' the Irish Cupcakes, 96
Marshmallow Fudge Sundae
Cupcakes, 70
Miss Pinky the Pig Cupcakes, 80
Peanut Butter & Milk Chocolate
Cupcakes, 60
Pupcakes, 91
Spider Cakes, 38
Cupid Cakes, 24

D
Dipping Sauce, 40
Doodle Bug Cupcakes, 84
Double Chocolate Chip Snack Cake, 64
Dough: Chocolate Cookie Dough, 14
Dough, Frozen
Cherry-Filled Hearts, 8
Crunchy Comets, 132
Snake Stromboli, 120
Dough, Refrigerated
Choo-Choo Train, 122
Christmas Tree Rolls, 50

Dough, Refrigerated (continued)
Coffin Cookies, 34
Holiday Candy Cane Twists, 50
Ice Cream Sandwich Hearts, 4
Luscious Lion and Lioness Cookies, 118
Moon Rocks, 128
Savory Sweetie Pies, 9
Skeleton Cookies, 44
Smashed Thumbsticks with Oily Dipping Sauce, 30
Snowball Bites, 46
Strawberry Hearts, 18
Sweetheart Pizzettes, 18
Zebras, 114

E
Earth's Core Meatballs, 138

F
Feet of Meat, 26
Festive Popcorn Treats, 48
Firecrackers for the Fourth, 98
Fish Bait with Gator Heads, 124
Fluffy White Frosting, 104
Flutter Away, 78
Flying Saucer Ice Cream Sandwiches, 142
French Fried Cacti, 150
Frostings & Glazes
Base Frosting, 17
Blue Cookie Glaze, 123
Creamy White Frosting, 17
Fluffy White Frosting, 104
Frozen Florida Monkey Malts, 112
Frozen Pudding Cups, 155

G
Galaxy Gel, 134
Giant Gift Boxes, 54

H
Holiday Candy Cane Twists, 50
Hot Dogs: Sloppy Goblins, 36

I
Ice Cream
Flying Saucer Ice Cream Sandwiches, 142
Ice Cream Sandwich Hearts, 4
Jack in the Box, 108
Ice Cream Sandwich Hearts, 4

J
Jack in the Box, 108
Jack-O'-Lantern Gingerbread, 100

K
Kittens and Mittens, 52
Kitty Kat, 86

L
Lacy Hearts Cake, 16
Ladybug, 76
Liberty's Torches, 102
Lime Chillers with Blood Drippings, 42
Lollipop Garden Bouquet, 33
Luck o' the Irish Cupcakes, 96
Luscious Lion and Lioness Cookies, 118

M
Marshmallow
Boo Hands Cupcakes, 106
Coffin Cookies, 34
Fluffy White Frosting, 104
Marshmallow Filling, 34
Marshmallow Fudge Sundae Cupcakes, 70
Marshmallow Filling, 34
Marshmallow Fudge Sundae Cupcakes, 70
Meringue Bone Cookies, 28
Miss Pinky the Pig Cupcakes, 80
Moon Rocks, 128

N
Nuts
Chocolate Almond Cherry Mix, 48
Feet of Meat, 26
Snowball Bites, 46
Space Dust Bars, 140

Nuts (*continued*)
    Sweet Mysteries, 62
    Topsy-Turvy Banana Crunch Cake, 68

O
Ooey-Gooey Caramel Peanut Butter
    Bars, 72

P
Peanut Butter
    Chocolate and Peanut Butter Hearts, 12
    Festive Popcorn Treats, 48
    Ooey-Gooey Caramel Peanut Butter
        Bars, 72
    Peanut Butter & Milk Chocolate
        Cupcakes, 60
    Super Peanut Butter Sandwiches, 149
Peanut Butter & Milk Chocolate
    Cupcakes, 60
Phases-of-the-Moon Toasted Cheese, 130
Ponies in the Meadow, 92
Popcorn: Festive Popcorn Treats, 48
Potato Bugs, 155
Pupcakes, 91

R
Raisins
    Cinnamon Cereal Crispies, 65
    Moon Rocks, 128
Raspberry: Ladybug, 76

S
Salmon Celery Trees, 144
Sandwiches
    Apple-Cheddar Panini, 148
    Phases-of-the-Moon Toasted Cheese,
        130
    Sloppy Goblins, 36
    Snake Stromboli, 120
    Super Peanut Butter Sandwiches, 149
    Toasted Cheese Jack-O'-Lanterns, 42
Savory Sweetie Pies, 9
Simple Molded Candy, 14
Skeleton Cookies, 44
Slam Dunk, 154

Sloppy Goblins, 36
Smashed Thumbsticks with Oily
    Dipping Sauce, 30
Snake Stromboli, 120
Snowball Bites, 46
Space Dust Bars, 140
Space Shuttles, 136
Spider Cakes, 38
Strawberry
    Chocolate-Dipped Strawberries, 20
    Cupid Cakes, 24
    Firecrackers for the Fourth, 98
    Strawberry Hearts, 18
    Valentine Smoothies, 22
    Wacky Watermelon, 152
Strawberry Hearts, 18
Sunshine Sandwiches, 66
Super Peanut Butter Sandwiches, 149
Sweetest Heart Cake, 10
Sweetheart Pizzettes, 18
Sweet Mysteries, 62

T
Teddy Bear, 82
Time to Party, 94
Toasted Cheese Jack-O'-Lanterns, 42
Topsy-Turvy Banana Crunch Cake, 68

U
Under the Sea, 88

V
Valentine Smoothies, 22

W
Wacky Watermelon, 152

Y
Yogurt
    Crunchy Peach Snack Cake, 58
    Valentine Smoothies, 22
    Wacky Watermelon, 152

Z
Zebras, 114

METRIC CONVERSION CHART

VOLUME MEASUREMENTS (dry)

1/8 teaspoon = 0.5 mL
1/4 teaspoon = 1 mL
1/2 teaspoon = 2 mL
3/4 teaspoon = 4 mL
1 teaspoon = 5 mL
1 tablespoon = 15 mL
2 tablespoons = 30 mL
1/4 cup = 60 mL
1/3 cup = 75 mL
1/2 cup = 125 mL
2/3 cup = 150 mL
3/4 cup = 175 mL
1 cup = 250 mL
2 cups = 1 pint = 500 mL
3 cups = 750 mL
4 cups = 1 quart = 1 L

VOLUME MEASUREMENTS (fluid)

1 fluid ounce (2 tablespoons) = 30 mL
4 fluid ounces (1/2 cup) = 125 mL
8 fluid ounces (1 cup) = 250 mL
12 fluid ounces (1 1/2 cups) = 375 mL
16 fluid ounces (2 cups) = 500 mL

WEIGHTS (mass)

1/2 ounce = 15 g
1 ounce = 30 g
3 ounces = 90 g
4 ounces = 120 g
8 ounces = 225 g
10 ounces = 285 g
12 ounces = 360 g
16 ounces = 1 pound = 450 g

DIMENSIONS

1/16 inch = 2 mm
1/8 inch = 3 mm
1/4 inch = 6 mm
1/2 inch = 1.5 cm
3/4 inch = 2 cm
1 inch = 2.5 cm

OVEN TEMPERATURES

250°F = 120°C
275°F = 140°C
300°F = 150°C
325°F = 160°C
350°F = 180°C
375°F = 190°C
400°F = 200°C
425°F = 220°C
450°F = 230°C

BAKING PAN SIZES

Utensil	Size in Inches/Quarts	Metric Volume	Size in Centimeters
Baking or	8 × 8 × 2	2 L	20 × 20 × 5
Cake Pan	9 × 9 × 2	2.5 L	23 × 23 × 5
(square or	12 × 8 × 2	3 L	30 × 20 × 5
rectangular)	13 × 9 × 2	3.5 L	33 × 23 × 5
Loaf Pan	8 × 4 × 3	1.5 L	20 × 10 × 7
	9 × 5 × 3	2 L	23 × 13 × 7
Round Layer	8 × 1 1/2	1.2 L	20 × 4
Cake Pan	9 × 1 1/2	1.5 L	23 × 4
Pie Plate	8 × 1 1/4	750 mL	20 × 3
	9 × 1 1/4	1 L	23 × 3
Baking Dish	1 quart	1 L	—
or Casserole	1 1/2 quart	1.5 L	—
	2 quart	2 L	—